RIGHT SIDE UP

How to Stand Upright in an Upside Down World: Spiritual Healing Tools for Manifesting Abundance, Self Empowerment and Personal Growth

Confessions of a Spiritual Rebel

Lane Keller

with
Jane Donovan

Copyright © 2024 by Lane Keller

All rights reserved.

No part of this book may be reproduced in any form or by any electronic or mechanical means, including information storage and retrieval systems, without written permission from the author, with the exception of brief quotations in book reviews.

ISBN: 978-1-941117-11-8

Library of Congress control number 9781941117118.

Contents

Preface	vii
Foreward	xvii
Acknowledgements	xix
Phase I: The Alchemy Within	xxi
Chapter 1: Inner Alchemy	1
Chapter 2: Real Life Magic	11
Chapter 3: Mindflips	18
Chapter 4: Magnetic Manifestation	26
Chapter 5: Soul Partners	34
Chapter 6: Creating A Magic Shift	49
Chapter 7: The Dimensional Spectrum	63
Chapter 8: Jumping Dimensions	71
Phase II: The Physical World	79
Chapter 9: Getting Off The Mountaintop	80
Chapter 10: Beneath The Veil	93
Chapter 11: Your Physical Self	102
Chapter 12: Health Freedom	112
Chapter 13: Living Unprogrammed Lives	118
Chapter 14: Honing Your BS Meter	121
Chapter 15: Banishing Limiting Beliefs of Yourself & Others	126
Chapter 16: Understanding The Dark	133
Chapter 17: Avoiding Further Traps	142
Phase III: Our Best Selves	149
Chapter 18: Incoming Abundance	150
Chapter 19: Personal Spirituality	159
Chapter 20: Exiting The 3D World	167
Chapter 21: Moving Into Mastery	179
Chapter 22: Unleashing Your Superpowers	185

Afterword	195
I Hope You Enjoyed This	197
Confessions of a Spiritual Rebel Series	199
About the Author	201
Other Works by Lane Keller	203
Two Gifts from the Author	205

This book is dedicated to my parents, Joyce and Jack Keller for being perpetual seekers of truth and wisdom. Thank you for sharing that wisdom with me.

Preface

You could call me a rebel. I don't really listen to anyone. I listen to my mom from time to time, but even that is debatable. There is a small handful of people on social media who provide good information whom I give credence to sometimes. I definitely do not listen to anyone positioning themselves as knowing it all, who charge for "ascension" techniques, who charge high prices for psychic readings, or to any so called "gurus."

I didn't listen in school, and I don't listen to schools of thought, particularly when it comes to spirituality. I have reasons for this and I'll share them as we go on. I don't attend spirituality classes and have not taken a course in ascension or manifesting—unless of course you count the time my mother enrolled me in Shelly Dumas' spirituality class in her basement in Syosset, NY when I was 12. Do I have the benefit of having been born to two incredible truth-seeker parents? Yes, I do.

They were on a trajectory of learning which I benefitted from. Their desire for information centered on spiritual growth and personal health. Through trial and error they came to look to the teachings of Edgar Cayce, Paramahansa Yogananda, the mystery schools revealed by Astara, Masters of the Far East by Spalding, and many pertinent others as the basis of their blossoming spiritual understanding.

My parents had no limits on their quest to understand the spiritual universe and our parts in it. The exception to this was anything fake, a deliberate ploy for money, anything unnecessarily "mysterious," or which had at its basis ego. There was their story of one well-known Spirit Guru and his channeler, whose "cult" has continued to multiply to this day, whose amazing information would be bestowed upon you once you forked over thousands of dollars. This was back in the 70's. The initial session was so rife with mind control programming that people were pulling out their checkbooks before session's end, except of course for my parents, who sniffed this sort of stuff out like suspicious bloodhounds.

There were psychic fairs, yoga camps, spiritual camps like Silverbell and Lilydale, and visits with every psychic within a 1500 mile radius of our home on Long Island. This foray into the supernatural taught me the immense value of discernment and of keeping your mind open—because the highest and most trustworthy info came from the most unlikely sources. A brilliant psychic named Irwin, for instance, whose skill at pulling out brilliant tidbits from the ethers was matched only by his very unpsychic family's gluttonous attachment to my mom's cooking. When Irwin first saw the Twin Towers being built some 28 years before their demise, he stuck out two fingers and lowered them with a whistle. "Down they come," he said, mimicking their eventual fall. The psychic adventures taught me the difference between light and dark. As young children my brother and I knew who was working in the dark and who was in the light. Emily, for one. A powerful psychic who excelled at giving bad news ranked high on our "we don't like her" list. We may not have always been able to put the reason into words, but we knew who not to trust. And we didn't trust the dark ones, or actually anybody except our own mom. For her powers were formidable, helping hundreds if not thousands of people find loved ones, connect with the departed, get married, or become pregnant. Of course her powers were mysteriously off when it came to us. "I see you becoming a biochemist," she said as I ran off to study drama at NYU. Well, maybe she didn't say that exactly, but you get the picture.

My parents questioned everything, as I do, and I question even their philosophies. I question the masters not because their wisdom is faulty but because the needs and understanding of humanity is evolving while our ability to assimilate and utilize information declines. We on this planet are going in many trajectories at once. Dangers are magnifying. We are in the midst of an all out war between light and dark, a war some may not even be aware we are in. Know it or not, we are engaged in the fight of our lives.

This book is not to spread fear. The more you know the better actions you can take. The more you heal your inner and outer worlds, the further you will go in helping to win this war. The fact that we are all here now is because on some level we chose to partake in the most epic battle ever waged, in which humanity, goodness, and the side of God, the Source wins.

Everything I have relayed in this book, all techniques, fixes, short cuts, wisdoms, and truths come from direct experience. I take no one's word as law and neither should you. Every bit of information must be sifted and held to the light for examination. To understand it, you need to feel it, and use it.

Let me repeat that, as it is a vital part of this book. *To understand it, you need to feel it, and use it.*

Words are cheap, as they say. What counts is whether or not something works, and whether it works for you.

You won't find any arbitrary repeating of concepts, truths or laws here, only methods that *work* that I have uncovered through real life experience and personal discovery. My guides, who stand by with answers, have helped assemble and define the ideas contained here. They are also the ones who urged me to write this book. A few months prior to writing this they made it clear I was to release a book clarifying spiritual concepts and to help people transform into their highest, best selves. The time had come, and I was to deliver this book in a clear, easy to follow, no nonsense way. But, I said, how on earth am I supposed to do this in—what? a couple of months you say?

My previous writings had taken far longer to complete. Some took years. My guides said not to worry, and sure enough it came together in the time frame they stipulated.

Sometimes my beautiful guides provide a straight downpour of information. I can get this to occur by asking a question then walking around the lake near my home with my dog and recorder. Words fly out as I dictate the answer.

Other times, like when I'm running a meeting, in conversation with someone, or as often happens, in the dream state, my guides deliver concepts through a single word. If this happens when I'm sleeping, I will bolt upright in bed and write it down. It's up to me then to discover the meaning behind the word and to expand on it. If I'm in a meeting and share a word or name I've just received, the people around me know to take this word seriously. Without fail, it will greatly expand or redirect whatever we're talking about.

I love that my guides join meetings with us. They know I love language and so this is sometimes a fun game that we play, as a completely unthought of word pops into my head at exactly the right time or in answer to this or that problem. It is always perfect.

You would recognize the names of some of these guides, but they prefer not to be named and instead call themselves *The Collective*. The Arcturians also prefer not to use individual names. The reasons for this have to do with humility and because they are part of unity consciousness. Ego requires names. Delivering profound information that helps humanity does not.

As you now know, my background might be considered peculiar. I stand as an iconoclast, although I have chosen at times to blend in. The reasons for this are similar to that of the Collective's. Information, vibration, truth—your brand of personal authenticity—are more readily accepted when you meet others at their level.

I am different in others ways as well. I can't be told something for I will not absorb or accept it. Instead I have to feel it. At first I thought this was due to stubbornness, but as I matured I became grateful for this tool that was soon integrated into my process. By *feeling into* a conceptual thought you can utilize it without effort. It is what I call assimilation: the absorption of information that becomes integral to your being. In other words, through feeling, concepts become part of your nature. This is not to put down analysis. As a writer/researcher I put great store in intellect and research. But when learning a new concept it is always best to feel it, in my opinion.

Everything found in this book comes from my own process, every single thing. It is not an amalgam of spiritual ascendance or awakening theory. It is the result of years of effort and integration, as well as distillation of complex ideas into simple truths. I use "effort" loosely because much of it flowed as I pushed forward in my pursuit of truth. I never knowingly embarked on the path of ascension, yet I have been on it since birth.

What I thought I was on was the perpetual quest for truth and authenticity. This was my driving force, coupled with the intense outrage I felt over injustice and harm done to innocents and good hearts. I dislike injustice in all its forms. I wont use the word hate because everything, absolutely everything has a spiritual, or let's say "unknown," purpose that you can uncover if you look hard enough.

This acceptance of the unknown order of things eventually integrates into your personality. This holds true for the other concepts shared here as well, such as how to embody humor, love, lightness, and joy. These are abstract concepts and can not be pursued on their own, nor should they be. They are instead the benefits of the path that drives you. Let me repeat that. Instead of pursuing "happiness," for example, pursuing the path of personal integrity and authenticity will provide happiness as a byproduct.

Is your path a quest for truth? Is it a path for justice? Maybe it is a path of self betterment. Maybe you are motivated by the desire to eradicate the dark. You will find your motivational force as you move forward, if you haven't already.

The way this book is written differs from others. It is not meant to be a highly organized and strict How-To. It flows and meshes and instead follows a river of knowing. It is a fun river I hope, as the ideas, some of which are repeated and presented in different ways, take hold.

As this occurs, what changes do they bring within? What bells go off as you land upon something that resonates with you? That resonance, when it comes, should be isolated and cherished. That is a leaping off point.

Read this book not as a primer or a textbook, but as a discussion. From time to time my interviewer, Jane Donovan's voice pops in, because many of these ideas needed to be solidified and isolated. Until such times as Jane helped bring them out there were hidden aspects of my being that I did not in myself recognize, for I had so integrated them into my personality they were difficult to pinpoint. In other words, my quest for truth, justice and authenticity had generated *self-development shortcuts* that I did not myself always perceive until the beautiful being of Jane pointed them out to me.

That being said, my quest has been a painful process at times, encompassing the dark night of the soul, that enormous wall of despair that threatens to engulf you until you come out on the other side. The most difficult moments spent with my twin flame combined with the discovery of the worst, most hidden, dark secrets of the shadow world created a tsunami of grief which marked a major turning point for me, or what I consider my true point of embarkation. In other words, this is where my journey really began.

As I travelled down to the pits of child trafficking, Luciferian worship, and demonic behaviors that entailed untold tortures of our most innocent, I wondered how the world could ever pull itself back up. I knew it would not do so without our help—all of our help. Instead of taking me down it quadrupled my conviction. I became indomitable. I refocused my direction into bringing awareness to these things. It has taken years of pouring effort into these ends. Some wrong turns—let's not say wrong, but detours—ended in what appeared to be dead ends. During this time I produced 60+ *Lane Explains* videos which were all taken down by the YouTube bots, *The Arcturians* and *Talking Galactic* with my mom, documentaries on child trafficking and FDA cover ups, created a network of truth-bearing documentary producers, and much much more. I have worked with various "humanitarian" groups who were as ostensibly set on creating the new media as I was, or funding the same. These groups did not turn out to be fruitful and some were downright harmful. I will say at least one was demonic, because the subterfuges the alleged leaders used could only point to dark forces out to subvert those trying to do good for humanity.

Eventually, and probably because of these episodes, I knew I had to stop relying on others, because that was what it was doing. I was aligning myself with those whom I wrongly believed had more to say or better ways of saying things than I did. Many of these individuals turned out to be very dark despite appearances to the contrary. This recognition was also part of my growth process. When I broke free of the last of these groups I knew I would never put my energy behind someone else again, but instead would forge forth, solely, if I had to, using my own voice and garnering what ever energies I could muster into the force for positive change.

At that time of breaking free several stalwart souls surged forward with me. They knew as I did that the time for change had come, and that we had the knowledge, tools and passion to help it transpire. LifeSource was created, and multiple trajectories shot off from there.

There is another faction that must be identified here, the Arcturians.

"You've got to choose," they say, meaning you've got to choose the side of ascension. Do you? Do you choose to live an authentic life that is free of harm to others or yourself? Yes? Then that is a choice.

For we create our own paradise, a world we were meant to have all along, a world that is right side up. The longer we are in a higher vibration, the more we get to associate with people vibrating at the same frequency, or in other words who are like us. The idea of experiencing love and peace all the time probably sounds boring. But ascension is merely a way of being that eliminates strife and unhappiness. It can be as exciting as you make it.

I've never yearned for peace on earth, exactly. I've yearned for truth and for people to awaken from this dream reality and to see who's creating the wars and divisions. To be over on the other side or in an elevated state, means you don't have to participate in the carnage but sometimes you still have to watch it.

Getting to more on how this book came about, in 2015 the Arcturians started delivering plans for a new world that included a new media, and a new way of being. Soon, they told me, it will be time to develop that blueprint as the world enters the new paradigm.

Before this can occur, however, the related philosophies and knowledge had to come out. This was to be the framework for the book.

What did I want the world to know? Jane then asked me, having heard the story. I said I didn't have a clue. "Yes, you do," said Jane.

I have the kind of brain that puts things into organizational patterns. But I didn't want to have to adhere to a limiting formal structure. So, I invited the Collective to speak. To help this along, Jane asked me questions. From there things opened up.

We went through many titles, the guides, Jane and I. *The Rising of a New Humanity. The Old Earth, The Characteristics of the Dimension We're Leaving Behind. The New Utopia*, and many more. It wasn't until they gave me, in true Collective form, the correct title—as usual, when I was thinking about something else.

Right Side Up, How to Stand Upright in an Upside Down World.

I realized that Phase I of this book would be creating the alchemy within. Inner alchemy is the transmutation of trauma and the things that are holding us back, such as self-sabotage and outside programming. Phase II would be opening people up to the realities of the physical world, or pulling aside the blinders that have shielded humanity and left them in a place of inaction for too long. Phase III would be utilizing these concepts and elevating into our best selves.

I read something interesting about Hermes, the ancient Egyptian who created the Emerald Tablets, the sacred texts written on green stone. He talked about the alchemical process, which some take to be about gold, but translator Dr. Matthew Barnes said, no, what it really meant was the alchemy within.

How do we create that desired alchemy of spinning straw into gold, shedding the programming, understanding what dimensions, vibration and frequency are, honing the perception, removing ego from the equation, and more? I didn't think I knew the answers but I knew that when they came they would be part of the collective change.

Then comes creating the desired alchemy without, beyond your body, beyond your physical self, beyond you. This includes awakening to the truths of the hidden world, and entering the new relationship paradigm, the new business paradigm, and everything else that is part of the plan for a new humanity. Then comes the understanding that will help skyrocket you into the higher dimensions.

Now readers, this is a special note for you. If at times you feel the information in this book is getting too heavy or too much to understand or too difficult to put into practice, do not worry. This book and these words are frequency based. Look at how homeopathy works. It is a treatment where the essence of the substance is distilled down thousands of times so as to be purely vibrational in nature. When you take the substance it causes the body to react in a way that eliminates the problem. It goes to work on the specific symptoms, getting down to the root cause as you go from remedy to remedy. This is classical homeopathy, not the kind you find in the supermarkets where the remedies are combined, which lessens their effectiveness.

This book operates in a similar fashion. It is pure in its intent. It is distilled down to the essence. Just read the words. Hold the book in your hands. Sleep with it under your pillow or in your bed if you desire. Let it seep into your consciousness. You do not need to take notes unless that helps you process the information. You only need to read the words. Let the words, your guides, and the Universe take care of the rest.

Thank you for taking the time to read this book. When you're finished reading please take a few minutes to write a quick and honest review on Amazon. I read every review and use the feedback to improve the book and future writings. If you haven't already please subscribe to my newsletter at LaneKeller.com where you can join a community of like-thinkers as well as free books and other goodies for signing up. Hold on tight now as you are soon to enter new realms and the fulfilling life you in your deepest being know is possible.

All my very best, Lane Keller

Foreward

by Jane Donovan

When I first met Lane, we immediately knew who the other was. Some would say it's that 'soul sisters' feeling, however it was more than that. We appeared to be a mirror to each other and as our time spent together grew, the synchronicities between our decades of living became greater and greater. While not being doppelgangers, we still to this day are incredulous at the similarities.

During this time, I had the pleasure of being on dozens if not hundreds of Zoom calls with Lane and the various production and project teams related to LifeSource. It was during these meetings that I started to see the differences between Lane and myself. I'll start by saying that often these meetings became passionate, sometimes triggering, argumentative and philosophical as they are filled with richly spiritual humanitarians. Many of them are the real doers of this world who are in a hurry to get stuff done. Others are philosophers or visionaries, some networkers, and others gentle earth angels. This melting pot of extreme personality types and passion can often be a recipe for chaos.

Lane directed these sometimes 3-hour long meetings with the consistent mastery of many qualities I admire and that are much needed in this world at this time. She navigated potentially tricky situations with grace, leadership, support, inspiration, solutions, and wisdom while holding a consistent high vibration. That's not an easy feat to achieve. And not once did I feel her being triggered. The woman appeared to have superpowers I didn't, and I wanted to know how she had developed these skills.

I have been fascinated by emotional intelligence since the age of 10 and I wanted to know how Lane became so masterful. I soon realized she had a combination of an unusual childhood raised by two very conscious parents, and the ability to quantum leap spiritual lessons. It would be easy to suggest that Lane had spiritually bypassed some lessons however as you will discover in the reading of this book, she hasn't.

My voice is minimal in the book however it appears where Lane has potentially made an assumption that her quantum leap is a doable thing for us all. I interject where I feel needed to gain greater clarity about the 'how' in some situations and I hope like me, you are fascinated by Lane's journey and wisdom that we all I know wish an abundance of in the world for us all today.

Happy reading, Jane xx

Acknowledgements

Writing acknowledgments for a book such as this is tough because the work has blossomed from knowledge gained over a lifetime. How does one pinpoint the influences in his or her life?

I gratefully acknowledge my parents for being wise and perpetual seekers of truth and wisdom and for sharing that wisdom with me.

I most gratefully acknowledge the highest teachers of all, God, or *Yahweh*, and *Yeshua*, also known as Jesus, the Planetary Logos, or "Brother," as he said he likes to be called.

I gratefully acknowledge the master teachers who continuously bestow their wisdom on the planet, including those whom I have been fortunate to connect with on a spiritual level including Edgar Cayce, Paramahansa Yogananda, Nikola Tesla, my own father in spirit, and the many others who form "The Collective."

Toward this end, I gratefully acknowledge the Arcturians and the wealth of interdimensional teachers who share their wisdom including Running Bear and others from the indigenous nations.

I gratefully acknowledge the teachers I read or came in contact with in my youth and early adulthood such as Ruth Montgomery, Dr. Raymond Moody, Brian Weiss, Baird Spalding, Kahlil Gibran, Delores Cannon, Alex Collier, David Icke, and many others. It is impossible to gauge how much influence these sources have had as all have contributed to the creation of a new paradigm of which I am most thankful to be involved.

I gratefully acknowledge Jane Donovan, who serves as an

interviewer in this book, and who is an insightful, motivational powerhouse in her own right.

Phase I: The Alchemy Within

> "First you have to get rid of the old junk.
> The garbage and the baggage
> out of your life.
> And then you can move into
> what you really came for."
> Delores Cannon

Chapter 1: Inner Alchemy

A lot has been written about achieving a higher vibrational state of existence. If you are familiar with the work of seers like the late great Dolores Cannon, you will understand that despite contradictory appearances, the world is on a path of ascendancy leading us to a higher vibrational state of existence.

What does the movement toward ascendency mean and how does it affect our daily lives?

In a high vibrational state of existence you begin attracting that which you positively radiate outward. As you begin to do this your ability to create what you desire increases dramatically. The people around you grow in harmony with who and what you are. You proceed on a career path that is joyful, motivating and which inspires your passion. This is because it is in accordance with your highest self and purpose. You greet everyday with anticipation because you are not facing drudgery, but instead look forward to inspiring, soul expanding endeavors.

As you move ahead in your new way of being you help others with your infectious laughter and high vibrational state. You automatically dispel that which is "dark," or not in accordance with your highest soul trajectory. Low energies just can't stick to you.

You readily attract members of your soul family. Your love and joy spreads as you feel the interconnectedness between all living things. This is not some hollow "we are all brothers" claim, but rather you feel the truth of connection on a very deep level.

You do not put yourself first but do not neglect yourself either. Your boundaries are secure. You are confident in who and what you are and do not require validation from others. You now carry within yourself the freedom to lift others to be their most bold, authentic, empowered, knowing selves. It is easy to be kind and uplifting to everyone you meet.

Forgiveness is not a problem for you, in fact you've moved past this into a state of thankfulness, and to even higher levels in which you love your experiences, all of them. Your body is healthy and on track to becoming youthful, supple and strong. You look good because you carry a confidence about you. You are grateful for the times you have with family because you've dropped expectations and are welcoming of everything that comes to you.

Money? That is part of the flow of your life. What you need you receive. God, Father Yahweh, Source, the Universe—the benevolent male/female Creator Force that guides our existence—will take care of you, as long as you create the conditions for it.

Love? Indeed so, and in very many forms. You love yourself and you love others. If you desire your true soul partner, then this union will come into being. If the partner you are with has stagnated then you will be able to help him or her move forward, or move on yourself. Learning who and what your sacred partner is, will bring him or her to you. This will expand as you radiate sacred oneness together.

Joy comes with the territory, because every moment is filled with love, blessings, connections and beauty. Then as you start to experience bliss and the truly wonderful aspects of being a knowing, sentient human, you will wonder why you never thought it important or attainable before.

Where to Begin

There are various books and courses that teach how to bring these beautiful gifts into your life. This book however, is different. Here there are no extensive workbooks, journals, mystifying talk, or lengthy procedures requiring years of study, not that anything is wrong with those things. Instead, with the help of some worldly and otherworldly friends, I share procedures that I have personally developed and put into practice over the years, often without even realizing that it was just a simple twist of thinking or a "mind flip" that changed things around. I thank my incredible spirit guides and my interviewer, Jane Donovan for insightful input and help in isolating the techniques that are, as she says, "Wait, stop there, Darling. That is surprisingly unique. Do you realize how unusual that is?"

You will see Jane's thoughtful questions intermittently throughout this book.

The Choice

Thinking back, I realize it begins with a choice.

It's a simple choice, not one you have to say aloud but one that you adopt within yourself. It is a choice that most fail to make despite thinking they have done so. This is the choice to be on the side of the light.

The unlit side, or the dark, entails ignorance, in-the-box thinking, restrictions, unhappiness, ignorance, unhealthy bodies and minds, selfish action, loneliness and even early death. It feels depressing, doesn't it? Yet millions of people choose this path everyday. Being caught in the medical/pharmaceutical/non-healing cycle is just one example of remaining out of the light. Dogmatic religion is another such trap. Believing politicians and false history are others. Thinking you are incapable in any way is another.

Sadly, indoctrinated thinking stagnates and suppresses these individuals, as does the idea of change. As various philosophers have said, we grow to love our chains.

What of the "Light" Side?

This entails being an alignment with Source, or God, or the

Universe or however you choose to define universal love, creation energy and goodness.

This choice for good comes with guideposts:

- To never stop bettering yourself (check)
- To never stop becoming all you can be (check)
- To never stop helping others and this world (check)
- To never stop choosing truth over lies (check)
- To never stop finding truth no matter how long it takes (check)

If this is you then you have just chosen ascension.

Ascension involves an inner transformation that brings about the outer one. The process doesn't need to be completed before changes begin happening in your life. Rather, they occur in increasing rapidity, eventually becoming so rapidfire you can not remember being any other way. Soon you can no longer remember what it feels like to be in a state of lack, shock, unhappiness or despair. As you deepen your learning, your outside world changes into the one you create.

You are about to turn your world right side up now. Are you ready?

Self Examination

How do we turn our inner world right side up when we are imbued with issues, traumas, and subconscious programs that are holding us back? Where does the change come in?

Let's say, "the unexamined life is not worth living." Socrates pronounced this before being sentenced to death for teaching the youth how to think for themselves.

This means you need to adopt the habit of examining your life at every moment of your existence. It is a way of being that you grow into. You can get rid of virtually anything, including trauma this way.

For instance you can eliminate those triggers that generate an involuntary action in you by following them to their root emotional cause. The same goes for body ailments. If you follow physical issues to their inception and examine the emotions you find there, you begin healing. You can learn to deal with people in an authentic way by examining the cause of your inauthentic behavior to the opposite. Self examination never stops and never should stop, because when it does you get runaway ego, illness and getting caught up in your own false story, in other words believing your own BS. This is opposite of being your authentic, true self.

Gurus and Elitist Thought

As for as gurus, self-appointed experts and those writing books like myself, LOL, thinking your stuff is better, more important or more enormous than someone else's will put you on the karmic path of being shown that it isn't. Our spirit guides and heavenly helpers are choosing to work through certain people on the planet at this time and many of us are speaking out. This can apply to you too.

Receiving information is awesome. It is transformative for both the receiver and the audience. It is important to remember that the information coming through each and every one of us is filtered through our individual ego. It's very rare to get pure information that isn't in some way colored by the receiver's level of understanding. This is why it becomes important to do it yourself. There is less error in translation.

Authenticity

Your examined life deeply inspects every aspect of your being and isolates what is not pure and authentic, then purges it. What in your actions or thoughts are coming from fear or damaged feelings?

There are people who are inveterate liars. They spill chronic lies every moment of every day, for no reason whatsoever other than it is easier to tell a lie to others and yourself rather than to be an authentic being. Your truth, your integrity—what happened to integrity? That's where self examination comes in.

Ask yourself: Am I being authentic to who I am, who I *really* am? Am I presenting myself in an authentic way and also taking the needs of the person before me, who's right here in this room with me, into consideration? The examination that goes on is perpetual, and leads us eventually into self realization.

Self Realization

We do work in our marriages, with our kids, in ourselves and we get to the point where we rise above the issues at hand and think we are done. But now we're talking about constant self examination. Socrates' student Plato went on to say that unexamined life is mere waste. This is the life that goes by without any realization. He talks of the nobility in one's self realization and that, "We humans are far better than animals, and so must use our sixth sense in developing ourselves to the supreme."

Self realization, according to 20th century prophet, Paramahansa Yogananda is "the knowing in all parts of body, mind, and soul that you are now in possession of the kingdom of God; that you do not have to pray that it come to you; that God's omnipresence is your omnipresence; and that all that you need to do is improve your knowing."

That knowing refers to both within and without. If a person chooses to live their life without examination, they would be ignorant of the effects of their choices on themselves and the people around them. It's important to make sure we're consistently dealing from a place of awareness, love and oneness, and not being reactionary or fearful.

We need to make sure we're not playing the victim, that we're not programmed. When we're triggered, what is that? It's an alarm bell, an undulating red flag waving in our direction. At these times ask yourself, *What's going on there? What is that cause of the reaction I just experienced?*

These are important steps leading us to fully realize ourselves on our path to unconditional love and authenticity. Without that you aren't really living. You aren't experiencing pure joy and will always be in some way unhappy. Without self realization you will not magnetize the things you really want to bring into your life.

With self realization you come to understand who and what you are and to relax into a state of being that leads to wholeness.

Rote Love Doesn't Work

A lot of people appear very loving and are doing so because the "good book" or some other source of authority says to do so. Some do good work out of fear of otherworldly retribution or worry about lack of heavenly reward. Others do good acts to convince others as well as themselves that they are "good" people. This is not why we should be loving. To truly evolve, you have to love unconditionally from the heart because you feel it in a pure, authentic way. This means acting when no one is watching or knows what you're doing. It means loving everyone, every living thing, and every organism. You must love it all, unconditionally and fully. Even the bad guys. You can disagree with their actions. If you find it hard to love them, surround them in a big pink heart bubble and send them off to Planet Lala in the hands of Source where they can do no further harm.

Connected Distance

We often say we're connected, but do we know it? Do we understand what it means? Do you know that what you experienced is actually what I experienced or what the guy on the street might be experiencing? Connection becomes a universe in which you can truly feel others as well as feel for them. We're moving toward a point where we will be able to not just acknowledge but to feel everyone's pain. There is a tightrope walk involved with this.

Empaths especially have a hard time with self protection. We need to empathize, but with emotional distance so as not to be hurt in the process. It is a skill to both feel and distance yourself from someone's pain, a skill that we're collectively learning. In fact we're on a huge planetary learning curve with this.

We've been learning both empathy and emotional distance through the various health crises as people around us make choices that entail living or dying. Yes, this is a choice, a subtly unconscious choice, spiritual or karmic in nature, and something on a certain level each individual opts for. We will be going into this in greater depth, as uncovering, examining and sometimes reversing these subconscious choices is integral to our growth.

Your Vibration

Next you need to examine your vibration. This doesn't have to occur every moment of every day, but at those moments you become aware of something being not quite right. Are people acting standoffish, hostile, unforgiving? It may be you. Check your vibration.

Are you down in the dumps? Depressed? Sad? What's causing those things? It's easy enough to turn it around.

Are you torn? Feeling neglected, lost, or despairing? You need to examine the emotional situation you find yourself in and make sure that you're not dumping it on those you come in contact with. It's not their burden. You need to work through it.

Don't Be an Energy Thief

Ask yourself in every moment of every day from every point of your being, are you shedding light and love and trying to operate from a place of consideration and grace? Doing so will raise your vibration nearly effortlessly. Ask yourself what the other person needs instead of you trying to get what you need. This refers to everyone you come in contact with.

Everything you say and do initiates a vibrational ripple that effects countless people. You need to be very aware of the words that you use and the manner in which you use them. It is all important. Be the light you wish to see, the vibration you wish to receive. This radiates a thousandfold. While it shouldn't be your reason for doing so, your effort will return to you in droves.

It's incredibly important to raise the vibration of everyone you're around. You should never leave anyone in a lesser state. You don't want to be an emotional vampire, as so many people are. Without even realizing it, they're sucking the energy and leaving those around them angry, confused or depleted. Not doing this entails setting your ego aside and putting others first.

Real World Discussion: Ego

Self esteem is saying to yourself, *I'm important. I'm smart.* Yes, you are. Ego is not just thinking that you're smarter and better than someone else, it's acting it out or voicing it aloud. You may be those things and more. But you're not more important than the next person. You don't even know what their true gifts are. Your neighbor could be a Ghandi in the making.

Our job as developing humans on this planet is to help people open their eyes to their true intrinsic worth, and for them to utilize this value.

It isn't our job to make anyone feel less than us.

This calls for setting ego aside. It's not always about you. In fact it's probably never about you. Instead, think about what you can bring to the table in this feast of upliftment. What information can you bring? What energies? What frequencies? That's what it's about. It's about giving not taking, putting others before yourself, but not in a way that's going to hinder you or box you in, or make you subservient or an accessory to dysfunction. Instead we need emotional and physical boundaries. Giving not taking does not mean accepting abuse of any kind.

That's part of the early growth process: creating boundaries. Healthy boundaries are vital to protect your physical, emotional and vibrational self.

Genius Tip: Seeing Vibration and Frequency

What is the difference between vibration and frequency? Frequency is external, meaning it's something that can be projected at or received by, whereas vibration begins internally. Vibration is your point of manifestation and magnetism.

If people could see energy, the world might be immensely different. If we could all readily see auras for instance, which is your frequency in color, and see how energy dances and interacts and flows, every conversation and interaction would immediately improve. Body language would be welcoming and supportive. Intention would become pure and agenda-free.

Start to envision energy.

See the colors you project and that others are projecting

toward you. See the waves. Deflect that which is negative and alter your own when they are not positive.

Harm none will become part of your being when you see the energy negativity generates. When someone yells and gets into a violent argument, for example, and you see how that energy physically wells up and moves into the other person's body, you will never yell at a living creature again.

Chapter 2: Real Life Magic

For me, it's comes down to one thing, one magical way of looking at things that changes everything and lifts your vibration. It's something that never fails and just —well it just works.

What is it?

You laugh. Yes, laugh.

You laugh at sleeping in and missing the train or that the car is not starting again even though it's raining and you just had it fixed. You laugh at tripping and bruising your tailbone, because you didn't break something at least. Murphy's law is funny. This is about perceiving the irony in things. It's about things turning out the opposite of how you've planned.

You know what happens when we make plans, right?

God laughs. The Universe generally has other things in store for us. In fact, the Universe and our spiritual helpers have a great sense of humor.

Train yourself to see irony. Irony is funny. The alternative is being pissed off or angry or stressed, and there goes your vibration: way down. This vibration brings more bad things to you.

So laugh instead, dammit, and mean it.

It's been laughter for me my whole life. Why? Because I want to lighten the load on not just myself but on others. Always. How do I do that? Use humor, as best I can.

Sometimes I'm not as funny as I want to be, but I'm always trying. I try to lighten whatever it is. If I'm in a car and I've just flown off the road and down a hill, which happened to me, as soon as you come out of the shock you make a joke or funny comment. It's because you're thinking about the other person's experience and the vibration you're transmitting.

Interviewer, Jane

Jane: Okay, wait, you've taken a quantum leap that most people haven't. So I want to ask you, how did you get to the point of caring so much about other people without being a people pleaser? Because that's a key point. Most people can't do that and we can't make the assumption that it's an easy thing for people to do.

Lane: That's part of the inner alchemy. Let's go back to examining. I've just slid down a hill and this happened to me when I first moved to Maryland with my then husband and the kids. It was a snowy Sunday morning, and I was off to meet them for holiday photos. I was probably rushing or not paying complete attention, and as I come out of a hairpin turn, I suddenly find myself flying over black ice. I went into a 360 degree spin and my car flew down an embankment sideways, landing exactly between two tall pine trees.

There was not an inch to spare on either side. I slid between them like a letter into an envelope, an exact fit.

So, first is silent shock. Then a man appears out of nowhere. An angel, I believe, and raps on my window, asking, Are you okay? He adds as I roll down the window, "Because a jeep with four teenagers went down that same hill a few months ago and three of the boys died."

I nodded to indicate that I was okay and said, "But something terrible happened. I spilled my coffee." Because the coffee I had prepared for myself that morning had splashed all over the dashboard and messed up my car. For some reason, I found that hilarious. Maybe I didn't want to think about those poor kids and what could have happened to me.

I know I'll be more conscious of turns and black ice in the future, but at a moment like this you need to laugh, and that's because I wanted to put the man at ease. I was thinking of him.

Afterwards, you have to examine it. Why did I fly down that hill? Perhaps that was my grandmother or one of my guides saying, Laney, you've got to slow down. Why did I land between two trees? Because I was not meant to leave the planet at this time and my guides and angels are working to protect me. The irony is the only thing I could think of in that moment was the spilled coffee.

So, examination is essential. Why did this happen? Why am I not dead? Thank you, God, is the thought. So is being thankful.

Jane: Is gratitude a big part of your life?

Lane: I'm sorry to say that I really dislike that word. I dislike it because it's on every mug, pillow, cute little plaque, and painted rock from here to Australia.

Gratitude, gratitude, gratitude. I dislike cliches in general because they lessen the impact of what the words mean. I feel that some fat cat globalist elitists are behind the gratitude agenda and pushing complacency on us instead of encouraging us to be all we can be. It sounds cynical, but I'm very aware of agendas. That does not mean I'm not highly, highly grateful, however, but that comes from me and not from a piece of crockery.

Jane: Okay, I get it. I totally agree. However, it does have a place as a valid tool in assisting people who are lower on the emotional ladder to like climb up to a better feeling place.

So maybe gratitude is useful as long as one doesn't stay in gratitude and continues to reach for a higher vibration of way of being.

Lane: I say instead, examine your life, examine every moment, and be thankful for the lesson. Thank God, thank the Universe. Ask yourself, why did this happen? And don't forget to laugh.

Using Karma to Your Advantage

In looking for the reasons behind our experiences we've got karmic life lessons being learned at every point. I took a big leap early on when I realized that we could probably lessen the karma we experience. I asked my guides, what if I learned my lesson right there on the spot, wouldn't that eliminate karma? So in my youth I started ascertaining the reasons behind my experiences and never stopped. I don't like creating karma and I definitely don't like experiences that become increasingly difficult until you've "received the message." The process of karma has my healthy respect, which is why I do everything I can to avoid it. Realizing this was a key moment in my life.

Another epiphany I had sometime later on was about fear. I stopped fear within a day—done and over. I will explain that a bit further on.

Back to using karma to your advantage. At the exact moment I was dictating this passage I dropped my groceries and decimated a dozen and a half eggs and my dented cans rolled down the driveway.

Why did that happen? Maybe my guides were delaying me for some reason. Maybe I just missed getting hit by a car.

So thank you, Universe. I'm very appreciative that you just saved me from something, whatever it was. Maybe I was simply to learn that I am not supposed to be doing too many things at once. Or maybe those eggs were bad. I take that onboard.

Universal Synchronicity: It's not what you think

There are many stories of people wondering whether something is a coincidence or some form of sign. I don't believe in coincidences. As soon as you say you don't believe in coincidences, everything changes. Here's another overused axiom I dislike: *Everything happens for a reason.* Yet it's true. I've said it to my own kids a million times. I even dislike my own voice saying it.

What's another way of putting it? Universal synchronicity. There's reasons for everything, including things that you cannot see. Once you know there's an entire world beyond what we perceive, then you know there's also a whole lot of stuff happening out there. There are universes of angelic guides, spirit helpers, interplanetary beings and much more. Many are reaching out to you at this very moment.

Jane joins the conversation.

Jane: A professor from Harvard School of Consciousness said maybe 20 years ago that if the Empire State Building represents everything that we know to exist, how much of the building do you think we are actually physically able to see?

So students guessed, oh, half of it, a quarter, etc. He answered that it was one grain of sand at the base of the entire building. That's what we physically can see versus what we know exists that we cannot see.

Lane: I don't know how that professor could possibly reduce human knowledge down to one grain of sand, because in fact, he has no idea of what we don't know.

Maybe it's a tenth of a grain of sand that we perceive. What I can say is that there is a tremendous world around us in very close proximity that is constantly interacting with us. It's not about seeing ghosts or detecting whether your grandfather is in the room. Rather, it's about understanding the moments of connection and delivery of information. These things will expand once you recognize them.

Their information is right at our fingertips. There's a couple of rules before getting there. First is to transform your thinking to accept that there are things we cannot see. And then moving forward, there is a sure footedness in saying, yes, I can make mistakes.

Jane: We all make mistakes. I don't make as many mistakes as I did before my dark night of the soul challenges. However, I strive to be as consciously aware of every move I make with dedication to come from love and not from fear.

Lane: I feel that it's important to acknowledge the path of least resistance. I'm not saying to avoid challenges or to take no for an answer. But when you are hit with obstacle after obstacle, it's wise to take a step back and ask, Okay, why isn't this working? What you are doing is probably not the best way forward.

If it's clear sailing all the way through and you're in the flow of giving and receiving, it's marvelous. You're flowing in the stream. The energy is rising. You're inspired. You've got new doorways opening up and new ideas budding. You're feeling great. That's how you know the way is right. You're feeling your way through it.

Your Soul Barometer

Emotions are the barometer of your soul. If it feels good, you're going in the right direction. If it feels bad, you're going in the wrong direction. Now this is presupposing that you are a good and moral person and not one who derives pleasure from the pain of others. That's a psychosis we do not fully address here. But what of people who derive happiness from other people's sadness? Then there are the people who take joy in stepping on other people.

These individuals are in fear and ego, fear of not being good enough and ego in thinking it's not coming back on them. It's time to do some deep soul cleansing.

Back to the barometer. This is the inner guidance that indicates whether or not you are in alignment with Source and the Highest Good. If a situation feels wrong or generates a negative emotion such as worry or fear, it most probably is wrong.

Self Esteem vs. Ego

Self esteem is not ego, at least not in the sense we are referring to here. Self esteem is rightfully knowing your skills, abilities and potential. If you don't know these things you will use your ego to make yourself feel superior in a false way. You might be 50 pounds overweight, but *Oh, look at that person. They're 60 pounds overweight.* Even though they've been dieting for months. *Lucky, I'm not as bad as them.* You're stealing somebody's joy with your energy.

This comes from a fear of not being good enough. Your ego kicks in and says, *yes, but they're worse,* and you pull them down so that you feel better. Instead use self esteem to boost yourself up. You are good enough. You are beautiful and perfect. Here's the key: you will never, ever get the full validation you seek from anyone else. It must come from you.

Like SNL character Stuart Smalley says into his mirror: *You are good enough. You are worthy. I like you.*

Put your need for validation away. Put others first. Build them up instead of yourself and just watch the magnificent resonance that occurs as a result.

Chapter 3: Mindflips

Simple ways of changing your way of thinking can bring about quick and effective change. These MindFlips reverse ways of thinking that are likely working against you.

Try reading them in a relaxed state, seated in a comfortable chair or on your bed. If you feel drowsy it is because you are moving into a more receptive state, which is ideal. If you fall asleep so much the better, as that becomes your processing time. When you wake up return here and read a few more.

MindFlip 1: Be a Magnet

Like attracts like. This statement holds very true for energy. Everything you put out there is reflected back on you. We will go into this in greater depth as we go on. Your moods, actions, and unsaid thoughts are picked up not just by those around you but by the Universe itself and returned to you. If you radiate a state of joy, helpfulness and abundance, the same returns to you tenfold.

Mind Flip 2: It Isn't Always You

I've said it before: we are not alone, and it's true. When you get clear information out of the blue, and it comes to you easily, it's probably not coming from you.

If you don't believe it, okay. There are people who have been completely unbelieving of the spirit world who still received tremendous messages and visitations. However if you give credence to what you are receiving, it makes it easier for your spirit assistants to transmit information to you.

It's important to recognize that there are benevolent forces around us trying to communicate in any variety of ways, at any given time.

MindFlip 3: Darkness, Begone

If you're getting evil, negative, or unsavory information, then you're on the wrong wavelength and you need to clean up your space. This means your inner space, your outer space—everything. If you are using a Ouija board, burn it. Are you in a place that's haunted? Cleanse and if possible, get out.

Are you using drugs and alcohol? Are you hanging around bars? Are you around people who are using negative symbology? Are you around people who pull you down?

Are you yourself negative? Are you depressed? Are you angry?

Are you in a place of perpetual dissatisfaction?

Any of these things can cause negative spirits to be attracted to you.

The dark is very real and it can have great power, but it's not as powerful as the light. It's important to deal with darkness and not be in fear of it.

First thing is cleaning up your space for physical, mental, emotional, inner body, outer body, and removing anything that is not 100 percent of the light.

Try this powerful technique for clearing out the dark.

When you are feeling something less than positive around you, thrust your arm straight out, palm facing outward, fingertips upwards, and in a forceful voice command, *I do not consent.*

Do it inwardly if you have to. Add, *Darkness, Begone!* Feel it in your being and repeat it until 100% effective. This works. Eventually you'll get to a place where you'll no longer have to say it, but just have to think it.

MindFlip 4. Substitute This for a Negative Reaction

The perfect time to use humor is when something happens and you experience an involuntary reaction in response.

How do you bring in humor?

When you experience something that places you in anger, frustration, disappointment, sadness, fear, or any kind of negative state, stop and become aware of that reaction. Then bring in the conscious thought of *how do I laugh at this*?

It just takes practice. Like anything else you're learning here, you've got to run a new tape. You could call it creating a new groove in your brain. This new groove is going to ultimately become second nature.

Back to the question: How can I laugh at this?

For me, it is super simple. Once I knew that negativity was feeding the dark side I flipped it into laughter.

As Monty Python said, "I scoff in your general direction." I think of this any time anything negative rears its head. They are far less potent than you when you are in your power. So take command of your power and forbid anything less than the highest vibration from coming near you and your loved ones.

MindFlip 5. Fear? Boom! Get rid of it

Think in terms of energy. Imagine two huge balloons. One is white, one is black. Every time you feed fear, the white balloon deflates and the black one inflates.

For me, it was an aha! moment when I understood that filling the black balloon provides *loosh*, the dark side's food. We know that all wars are bankers wars, that wars are deliberately created to bring about a money stream, but it is also to create loosh, or negative energy. The same holds true with poverty, starvation, disasters, and other inhumane conditions. They all create loosh. However you choose to think of those who bring harm to humans and the planet, know that your strife is the energy that feeds them.

The more we're feeling distressed, depressed, and fearful, the more the other side loves it. Me being a very stubborn individual, I am in not going to feed that process. I say, *Nope. Not happening.*

Take a day, just one day. Every time you feel a rise of fear, say *Nope. Not happening.* Fear can come in the form of anything. *Oh, a bill just came due. Another bill! How am I going to pay that bill?* Boom. That was fear. It feeds the dark side. Boom. Get rid of it.

I want to feed the high side. I want to make the good side nice and fat. I want the white balloon to inflate and to create billions of other filled white balloons. That means I am going to say, *Ha, I scoff at this bill, God will send me the money.*

MindFlip 6. Still Got Fear? Examine It

Fear can be examined at a deeper level. When bills come in and your immediate response is, *Where am I going to get the money from?* What is your fear? That you won't have enough money. That you are not abundant. That you are going to have the electricity cut off or no food on the table, etc.

Now look at it closely. Is it a realistic fear or is it a false fear? For most situations it's going to be a false fear. What if it's not false? What if the doctor has just given you three months to live? First of all no doctor is God that I know of, and without taking free will, level of determination, and self help measures like emotional cleansing, natural treatment, and spontaneous, miraculous healings into account, no one can determine your life span. Instilling fear at a very vulnerable moment under the guise of "facing reality" becomes a huge test as to whether or not you can combat fear. I suggest you ignore all negative prognoses you or your loved ones receive in life, and determine your own course.

Many people have come back from the brink of fourth stage cancer to full health. What trait do they share? Belief in their ability to overcome. Belief that a Higher Source will help with this.

With every rush of fear know it's time to try something new. For most people, it's going to be reminding yourself that you've actually always had food in the fridge and that your electricity has never been shut off, except maybe that one time you forgot to pay the bill. Remind yourself that anything, even a dire disease, can be overcome. Will fear help? No, it will make things worse. For what you put out there you attract in manifold ways.

Is it a real fear you are experiencing? Even if a criminal is chasing you down a dark alley your answer should be no, because fear can lead to panic and irrational action. A calm head free of fear will allow you to find options. So instead reframe the fear that's saying *I haven't got the money; I'm sick and scared; he's going to catch me*, to become:

All my needs are taken care of. Because that actually is the truth.

Enter Jane.

Jane: What we're talking about here is a false truth running the fear narrative.

Lane: When it happens you need to examine that and turn it into a true truth. Take out fear, and hold it up to the light. What do you see? Where did it come from? Who started this lack of belief in the abundance of your life?

Tell yourself, this fear is unreasonable. Fear will accomplish nothing, except bring more stress into your life. Fear is a hotbed for negativity, a petri dish full of premature aging and disease. It creates a pall of negativity that affects your well being and that of others. Do you want this? I don't think so.

So say *goodbye fear*, then go deal with the problem in a calm, productive, and empowered frame of mind.

MindFlip 7. Yes! to the Flow

Say you're holding a crystal wine glass really tightly, what's going to happen? It's going to explode. But if you balance it lightly between two fingers it'll balance there allowing you to sip it nicely. This illustrates the law of flow.

If you see a bill and your first rise is fear because your parents were fearful of bills and you even had times of living in your car, it stops the law of flow. Take a step back and breathe. Say a prayer. Ask God or your angels for assistance, then let it go. Put the situation in their hands then go sing a song or play with a child. Take a walk and look at birds.

There, you've just started the Flow.

MindFlip 8: Money is Energy

Start thinking of money in terms of energy instead of numbers. Money is not real. This currency we've been living with for the past 150 years or so isn't backed by assets. It's what they call fiat. It's fake. There is nothing behind it except air, greed and printed paper.

Money is not even in your bank account. What's there are numbers and decimals. The fractional reserve system calls for banks to hold only 20 percent of your deposits in reserve. They then loan you back your money with fees and interest. If the banks collapsed tomorrow the FDIC's promise to insure accounts up to $250,000 would disintegrate. There is not enough value in the system to repay everyone's money.

This is not meant to instill fear, only cautious knowledge.

What is money, in reality? It's energy. I'm going to give the guy who came to fix my deck $300. Yes, it was really only worth $200 and I could have bought food or a new tire for my car instead, but now he can feed his pet rooster and I've hired an assistant for a day. By saying, *Universe, thank you for providing the means for me to share this money*, it comes back to you in one form or another.

Maybe you stand to get evicted and you will not be able to pay your energy bill. Turn it around and put it in the higher power's hands and say *I know this will be taken care of. Thank you*. In fact, how about I call the energy company tomorrow, even though I've already asked for extensions and ask them to put me on a better payment plan? Maybe because you released it into the Universe's hands the person who picks up the phone will help you out one more time.

MindFlip 9: Call on Your Spirit Helpers

I want to touch on the positive entities helping from the other side. They are here to help us if you call on them. Surround yourself in white light first, and in the energy of the Creator.

There are a few people out there charging for psychic readings who say things like *so and so is about to die*, or that your partner is going to break up with you, or that you are going to experience something awful. In my experience in dealing with the other side, they never say anything negative. They only give positive, actionable information. I either get very clear direction that's not cloaked in fear, or they remain mum.

Jane: Do you want to talk a little bit about that? Because I think it's something that people need to know.

Lane: There has never ever been a dark prediction issued by the other side by your guides. If they do it's a malevolent force coming in or you're with an inexperienced practitioner who's misinterpreting. What the guides would say is, be more aware when you drive, or, you're driving too quickly. Make sure to wear that safety belt and you should also check your brakes.

They would never say you're going to get in a car accident next week. It's not the way the Universe works. They're not allowed to interfere with karma, and the guides are never going to give you a negative pronouncement.

MindFlip 10: The most Important Thing You May Ever Hear

This is my favorite saying and it's a law. There are no absolutes. Everything can be changed because we have free will. My mother and I go back-and-forth on this. She is prompted to give predictions. Then she says predictions can be changed. I respond, "Then why are you giving them? Don't give them."

My mother's skills have been in part focused by producers who demand predictions and audiences who came to expect them. While predictions are amazing at times, the practice rubs me the wrong way because anything and everything can be changed. It feels like a dog and pony show to me. Predictions come down to individual free will.

Jane: I've had a situation where I was getting guidance for a client. I just received a message of, your brother would really be a lot happier if you reconnected and spent some time with him soon. It turned out that the brother died not long after.

I share that as an example because they're not going to directly tell me something horrible. Oh, your brother's about to die. They're not going to instill the fear. But what they're going to do is put love in, which is go and spend some time with your brother. She was given the gift of guidance to do so. When her brother did cross, she was very grateful that they'd had that time together.

Lane: Beautiful. Psychic readings are in the hands of the interpreter. Information is only as good as the reader and most everyone is highly influenced by their own thoughts and opinions. It's a rare individual who can put aside their thoughts and be a true channel.

Even then, channeling is suspect. This was never more obvious than during the whole channeling debacle that happened within the New Age movement. This was when inaccurate streams of information were deliberately fed to channelers that led the population down the path of false light.

The situation has been somewhat cleaned up after channelers became aware of the infiltration and took extra steps to guard against false light coming through.

Let's say that predictions can change so it's best to focus on trends and energies, and things that need to be addressed. When COVID began, I asked my mother how long the pandemic was going to last and she answered, three years. I was horrified and said, "no! it's all going to be over in six months." Instead it lasted exactly three years nearly to the day.

The point here is that our helpers from the other side can supply us with information that acts as a very real outcome if you don't take steps to change it. In my opinion the public accepted the quarantines and fear-mongering talk related to lockdowns, and the pandemic did in fact last three years.

Chapter 4: Magnetic Manifestation

It is liberating to step into the flow of magnetized manifestation. Information is energy. Creation of your heart's desire is energy. According to one of the world's greatest minds, Nikola Tesla, *everything* is energy.

How does energy work, and more specifically, how do you harness energy to work for you? First, it's critical to discern the difference between the positive and negative energies that are being directed at you every day.

Instant Energy Reading

When you feel uplifted you can sense a shift in your vibration that is moving you towards something that will be good for you. Most people who are aware of the energetic nature of things know that if something you're reading or hearing brings on fear, dread or hopelessness the information is not just inaccurate, but deliberately designed to bring about this sort of reaction in you.

Let's talk about news and information coming at you through word of mouth, the internet, TV or some other medium.

Even moderately bad news when understood through a spiritual lens shouldn't agitate you. If this happens it is a clue that something dark is at work. In the media we call information that is deliberately meant to rattle you or bring on some kind of negative action or thought process, "fear porn." This can come at you through friends just as readily as news broadcasts. There are ways of coloring things that bring on a sense of dread, just as there are ways of presenting them in a hopeful, uplifting way.

At the other end of the spectrum, *hopium* is meant to give you a false sense of hope, or a belief that something other than yourself is going to create the desired outcome. This shifts our actions into low gear, because we think we don't have to do the work ourselves. This is far from the truth, and hopium, due to its falseness also comes from the dark side of things.

On the other hand, there are clues to positivity that you can tap into.

If it's a pure form of energy and information, it'll come to you with no barriers and will just flow. It's a type of knowing. Sometimes it's an answer to a question you have now or had in the past.

If you've seen the Arcturian shows I do with my mom, you'll see that when I'm in her presence I am much more able to receive and can get instant answers.

It's an instant knowing. She raises the vibration so high the spirits flock to us and the channels open up.

The other thing is that whenever I tap into a divine pure loving spirit, I start to cry. This happens without fail. I have to hide it at times. My eyes start to tear up and I get all choked.

Jane: I know when I'm delivered information that I get the goosebumps.

Lane: Yes, to add to the goosebumps, there's a flash of electricity. It's like you just got a little jolt. Yes, a good jolt.

Jane: All tingly.

Lane: The other thing I want to add is that whenever I manifest something a bit crazy, like something I really want and it happens, it just moves me up one more pin on the ladder toward the whole thing coming together.

Jane: What whole thing is that?

Lane: It's a divine connection between all things, all experiences, and all knowing. It's so large that I can only just put my finger on it. With every manifestation and confirmation, I get a little bit closer to understanding how large this whole thing is. It's huge. I can feel it and it is sublime.

Jane: When I share my thoughts about things I'd like to have happen, most people say, you're kidding, there's no way you can manifest that. I'll say, I just did. I did it by talking about it as though it's here.

I giggle like I'm five years old when I manifest something special. It's hilarious. I'll get a phone call saying, Hey, here's this opportunity for you, blah, blah, blah. And I just break into giggles. It's a playful joyfulness. I think a lot of the time we've lost that pixie fun, cheeky, playful energy. It feels like you're playing with the Universe and winning.

Lane: The more you recognize synchronicities and responses to your manifestations, the more they will come, because we're in the law of flow. It's just flowing. I don't get the giggles, but what I do get is complete confirmation that the Universe exists.

Not only does it exist, but that there's a higher power, and they're here, right now, with you. When something seemingly small happens, and it's in synchronicity, it's them merely telling you that, yes, we're working on the bigger stuff, but maybe it's not the right time for it. Maybe it's not quite right for you, and we need to tweak it a bit. Or maybe that individual that you're looking for is not here yet. We have to create him. There may be all sorts of reasons.

I do have to share the dog manifestation. This one is good because it's not huge, but it was big enough for me to take a step back, a big step back, with the other things I was trying to manifest at the time, saying, oh, okay, they're working on it, the other stuff just may not be here yet. My previous dog, who was my spiritual protector, was a little white Maltese named Spartacus. I loved him beyond measure. He was 10. 4 lb exactly, fit in my purse, and I could take him everywhere, especially in Manhattan, which was not particularly dog friendly.

I would place him in my purse, and he went everywhere with

me, traveling around the country, living in different states. There was a lot of walking, and we were deeply communicative with one another. He got extremely ill, and hung on till the end, probably a year or two before he could have left. When he did leave this earth plane, I asked my vet, who was holistic, how to prevent this from happening again.

Because Spartacus had barely lived ten years, and while he took on so much, some of it could be attributed to the genetics of inbreeding. My vet said, look, this is what you need to do. First of all, find a dog before he's been vaccinated. Secondly, put him on a raw diet. And three, no pure breeds.

I asked the universe to please send me a pup who is hardy, but that I also needed him to be the same size as Spartacus. I searched to find a dog who had not yet been vaccinated and after several months of combing websites I found a terrier mix puppy on Craigslist. The owner showed me his DNA report. He was Yorkie, Jack Russell, Pomeranian, and even a little pit. I convinced her to let me have him before they had vaccinated him telling him that I would be taking him to my vet, which I did. A year later, when he became full grown, what was his weight?

10. 4 lb. And he still is. He's pure black and the other was pure white. So that makes me cry because I know he is a divine gift.

Jane: That's so beautiful. And that's spot on. There's just no mistaking it. Shall I say my favorite manifestation story?

It didn't happen to me. It happened to a friend of mine, a beautiful woman who's on the other side. Now, many years ago, she wanted to open up a healing center and she had many courses. She taught inner child therapy and energetic healers, all sorts of things. She was a wonderful indigenous Australian woman, and she needed at the time 15,000 Australian dollars to open up her center.

And it wasn't happening. She was just not getting the money together and she became really annoyed and frustrated at the Universe. She said, if you really want me to do this, I demand this money now. A short time after she gets her bank statement and there's 15, 000 in her bank. And she laughed at the Universe and said, okay, I get it. Thanks very much. That's not my money, but I do get your sign. Thank you for that.

So she goes to the bank, which was one of Australia's largest and said, look, there's been a mistake. There's 15 grand that's been put in my bank and it's not mine. They said, okay, leave it with us. She then gets a phone call and they said, look, we can see that this money isn't your money, but we can't see where it came from. Our rules prevent us from taking that money out of your bank account unless we know where it came from. So it's your money.

She said, well, look, that's all well and good, but I don't want you coming back to me in three years time saying, oh, we found where the money goes and you owe us 15 grand. They said, no, we've actually really researched this. We cannot work out where it came from. They gave her a letter that said it was her money. She got her 15 grand and opened up a healing center. She's helped thousands of people over the years. I think that's one of the most beautiful stories of getting out of the way of the how.

Lane: Oh, that's wonderful. We think that we want something and then we've got to look at the steps to take to get there. It's important to take actions that maintain the vibration to be a match for manifestation. That was a great example of getting out of the how it's going to happen phase.

Everything was in alignment. She was obviously meant to do that, or it was in her blueprint, if you want to say a soul blueprint, where she was supposed to have that center. But it was her doing. She asked for it. It was her free will. The timing was right, and everything fell into place.

Because I do think timing is a big part of manifestation. It just doesn't always happen exactly when you want it to happen, or in the manner that you expect it to happen. The other thing I want to say about manifestation is, it seems like when you say it in a very clear and concise, and almost offhand manner, Oh, *I love having a little dog who's exactly the same size as Sparty*, it works better than any other way.

It needs to be very clear, very concise, very easy instructions to follow. I didn't write it on a note and stick it in my wallet. I didn't do a mantra every day. I may have said it three times. I'm not putting down mantras, but I think that often when people are manifesting, they actually get attached to the idea of not having it, meaning they are so used to not having it that lack begins to feel as comfortable as your favorite bathrobe.

Yearning doesn't count because that's more not having. What you want is grateful acknowledgement that it is already done, even in an offhand way. Detach from the results before fear or doubt kicks in, as in, *what if it doesn't happen? I really need this to happen.*

Jane: That's where if you detach, as you said, you very simply said what you wanted and detached and went about life. If you're holding the glass, you're holding the glass too tightly. *I'm grateful for this*, not that *I would need this*.

Lane: Perfect. I hope most people know by now you have to get rid of the words need or want, because neither belong in your vocabulary.

It's telling the Universe that you don't have something. I learned early on in my youth to banish the words, *no, I can't do this. I can't imagine this. I can't have this.* They don't belong.

Get rid of them and get rid of the word no when it's directed at the self, as in no, you can't have that. No, you're not worthy or no, that isn't for me. There's a million reasons for no. There's only one necessary for yes, and it's bigger than all the no's combined. As you evolve, you'll never again say, I want or I need. Instead, say I like, I appreciate. I want is selfish, and I need creates a lack that the Universe will respond to by increasing that lack.

Jane: You're putting it into the present tense. Of course the I am in capital letters is pretty powerful big statement too.

Lane: Yes, I also like past tense. Thank you for sending that blah blah blah.

Jane: That's very powerful. Yes. And then you relax and let go and realize it's already done. It's happened. You just don't know the timing.

Lane: It's here. Move on. Thank the Universe. And then the Universe will fill in the gap. That's the law of flow and giving the request space to occur. Chances are it will come. Chances are it will come when you least expect it or, funny enough, when you don't need it or don't want it anymore. Then you're like, um, thank you. They were waiting for you to evolve to a point where you didn't need it.

Interdimensional Humor

I almost feel like the delay in manifestation is some sort of universal joke. Hilarious. You have to understand that Jesus, Source, the Universe—they are all very funny. They have a good sense of humor. The Arcturians are funny. They may not have exactly the same sense of humor as we do, but they like humor. Once I tried to get the Arcturian I was speaking with to share his name. He said he couldn't because there would be no way for me to pronounce it. If you know me then you know I find it hard to resist a challenge like that. I pressed on. *C'mon, try me. I'm sure I can do it.*

Hahaha.

It was a completely unpronounceable and unrelatable sound. We don't even have the letters to capture it. It was hilarious and of course there was no way to reproduce it. He gave it to me anyway. They are good sports.

Jane: I think you're onto something incredible with this humor. I'm not really sure where and how, but I'm on board. I've never heard anybody talk about it, except I think years ago, Esther Hicks talked about the healing of the power of humor and healing of cancer.

Lane: It is part of who I am, but yet it's not a character trait. What is the character trait is wanting to put the other person at ease. That's where it comes from, and from finding great value and humor in writing or public speaking, because not only does it lift the vibration, but it puts the audience or other person at ease.

Humor is the great equalizer. Rich or poor, downtrodden or privileged, authoritative or not, humor puts us on a level playing field. It opens the doors to learning. It's a way of instantly slipping someone into the alpha state, where they'll be more receptive. In any case, it's just fun. If you can use humor, people will let down their sensors and relax into things. Oh, we're going to have fun here, and this isn't going to be a science lesson. Or, oh, phew, I thought this was going to be harder. Then the alpha waves roll in that allow receptivity.

Jane: As you're describing it, I can just feel that energy of humor. It's something that, as I said, I've not heard of before.

However, I think you're really onto something special because it's also accessible to everybody.

Lane: People are just so serious, including me. I mean, I get on those, I don't want to say rants, but if somebody opens the conversation and they want to know about something, I'll go there.

Jane: I think it's great. You're really opening up pathways and clarifying this humor thing.

Lane: As I've mentioned before, I think it comes down to irony. If you look up the definition of irony, it says, the expression of one's meaning by using language that normally signifies the opposite. Typically for humorous effect.

Jane: It's not like sarcasm though, is it?

Lane: No, and I do dislike sarcasm. It feels nasty. Irony is observing what's upside down about the situation. Not, I just lost control of my car and slid down a hill, but rather, I spilled my coffee. That's it. We're in an upside down universe. Coffee should never be spilled if one can help it.

Chapter 5: Soul Partners

I once brought the concept of the divine feminine up to one of my millennial friends and she responded, what's that? At that moment I realized there wasn't a concept in the minds of some young people of what being female was, much less in the divine sense. Since that time genders and the idea of the divine feminine as well as that of the divine masculine have become even more convoluted and buried under a heap of distortions.

A lot of this has to do with identity politics and of the destruction of the family being engineered by Tavistock and other institutions. This is covered in greater depth later on in the book. You can fight the concept if you want, but the mixing up of what constitutes male and female in their purest form, is a deliberate attempt to confuse the genders.

This does not put down those who are trying to establish their personal gender identity. In truth we're hybrid human beings. We're a mixture of all sorts of things. If you were a female in your last lifetime and now you're born a male, you might be imbued with one or another gender despite your physical form. If you were born feeling like you are in the wrong body then that feeling is something to be explored and very possibly embraced. The indigenous cultures valued those of mixed genders because they were thought to have the highest traits of both sexes.

The Divine Feminine

What exactly is the divine feminine? It is the embodiment of the qualities that define femininity in its highest capacity, such as fertility, intuition and creativity. It is right brain oriented. As I mentioned, we are hybrid beings. Men can embody divine feminine qualities every bit as much as women. This does not make men less masculine. On the contrary, embodiment of both the divine feminine and divine masculine indicates the highest level of evolvement, no matter which gender you are.

The divine feminine means loving all unconditionally. It means caring for all unconditionally. It encompasses those aspects that are traditionally applied toward being female in a powerful way. It's not meaning to be a docile pushover or to live without set boundaries. That's not femininity. The divine feminine is loving, caring, nurturing, and strong. The divine feminine gives life. It perceives truth in its entirety. In its toxic form it is smothering, overly emotional, people pleasing, needy and subservient.

The Divine Masculine

What is the divine masculine? By the same token, the divine masculine embodies masculinity in its highest form. This entails protection, action, leadership, discipline, logic and typically left brain thinking. Positive masculinity, for instance, employs strength, vitality, and testosterone in a non-aggressive, and unselfish manner. When the masculine becomes overabundant in aggressive qualities and moves toward controlling, warring behavior, it becomes toxic.

As of now the divine feminine is rising and the world is coming into its feminine, nurturing state. Love and compassion is being put before acquisition of money and power. We are moving toward a paradigm where we do not get ahead in life by lying, cheating, or stealing, but rather through loving consideration of the individual through the evolved qualities of the divine feminine.

Manifesting Partners

Can you manifest your divine partner? If so, what qualities should that individual embody?

When you think about manifestation, it isn't a bad idea to make a list and write out exactly what you need, and to be very specific.

But when manifesting who and what you desire, you have to hone in on the exact qualities you need. I zeroed in on this through the years, especially after I went through that destructive relationship with my twin flame that nearly killed me.

His controlling behavior nearly brought me down, but instead I emerged stronger. When I met him, I thought he embodied all I desired in a mate. Apparently I forgot a few things on the list. As you grow, you need to refine your requirements further and further, until isolating those things that are not just essential to your happiness, but essential to a fulfilling partnership with another being.

Jane: In the beginning, it was a long list.

Lane: You told me one day, you've got to change some of that. I kept looking it over and said, I can't, I can't. He has to be taller than me, for instance. I simply cannot make love to a man or lie in his arms who's physically shorter than me. I don't like it. And everything else was mandatory. He has to be funny, he has to be intelligent, or I will not feel challenged. His heart needs to be huge and his emotional baggage mostly healed. I don't want it to be a tutoring session where he's my student either. Instead, he tutors me as much as I tutor him.

In other words, questing and growing together. To me, that is essential. He needs a passion for life and for our relationship. He needs to enjoy giving as much as receiving. You'd be surprised how many men perform sex perfunctorily or as a conquest and not as an intimate connection, and most simply do not reciprocate. This was vital as well.

He needed to be more athletic than me so he could help get me out of my hermit like writing mode every once in a while. So, on and on and on. Oh right, and one last thing, he needed to be out of the Matrix.

Jane: That one's almost impossible.

Lane: I know, and last I said, okay, okay. I'm not going to presume what he looks like. Any preconception on my type, I let go. It's just not important. I said, Universe, send him. So then he came.

Jane: There's a big thing in there when you said it's not important what he looks like.

Lane: Black, white, gray, brown, short hair, long hair, no hair. I said, Universe, surprise me. And you know what? It did.

Jane: Can I tell you that 99. 9999 percent of women could not say that. So when I said you need to examine that list and reduce it, you reduced it by 99.9999 percent on that one thing. You went for what is important versus what you perceive to be important. And this ties in with many of the topics we've spoken of, which is that you have a unique way of looking at things that differs vastly from others, even those in this field.

Lane: This is a program where specific looks have been fed to us as to what is attractive. It's why so many have body dysmorphia. It's impossible to measure up.

Jane: Advertising's been telling us 20 million times per second every single day what should matter. The programming goes into who we should and shouldn't be attracted to, and yet you have to let go of dozens and dozens of programs in that one statement.

Therefore, you opened up a massive door of who could walk into your life because the thing that the elite, the controlling programmers want to have happen is for us to run programs that make it hard for us to connect with our soulmate or partner or whatever term you want to give it. In essence, they have stopped the masculine and feminine divine from uniting and doing their dance together.

Lane: And when doing that dance, you become infinitely more powerful. Being with a divine partner causes our ability to manifest to explode. That is the very last thing they want us to know. The program has run very deep to make sure that meeting your true partner doesn't happen in life.

Jane: Yet, you've just thrown away that program that has the greatest success for them in one smart move.

Lane: Okay. So then the rule is don't define appearance because love defines everything.

Secrets to Soul Partner Manifestation

When isolating the characteristics your ideal partner possesses it comes down to self knowledge. You must define the essential qualities that have nothing to do with preconceptions, but are that which you find vital on a very deep soul level.

I could not have done this in my twenties. I was looking then for somebody who would be a good provider and a good dad. That's part of evolution, as women want to safely have babies. Obviously we needed compatibility along with basic things like laughter and intelligence. But he also fit a concept of what I thought would reflect well on me. I wonder now how much of our initial attraction was predicated on unimportant parameters. Did the fact that he fit my concept of who I wanted to marry "allow" me to fall in love? This turning point defined the next passage of my life in which I was mislead by programming in a number of areas. These were not choices I regret making, but ones that bear examination.

When trying to define your ideal partner at whatever stage you're in, you have to drill down to the bare basics and isolate the things you absolutely cannot do without. Then you have your list.

What else went away of mine? Money. I decided I didn't really care about money, not at this level. I did in the beginning because of the baby-making thing. As I matured I wanted somebody who was self-realized. To be financially dependent is not good emotionally for either partner, and can lead to deep issues, so financial self-sufficiency was important.

The point is, get that list down to exactly what you need then examine it some more.

Maybe as a woman you want somebody who embodies the

divine masculine. To have somebody who is secure in his own self and who stands in his own shoes, so to speak. Meaning he's secure in his being.

As a man if you want someone who nurtures you and feeds your body and stomach then what you are in need of is a mother. You'd better take a hard look at that. If you are a male seeking a divine partnership then it's time to dig deep. This soul searching quest speaks to emotional maturity. How mature are you? What do you really need in a relationship? If either party wants someone they can control then that speaks to immaturity. You can't find a partner in somebody who's weak and who can not stand up to you.

Of course there are moments when you want the other person to take the lead, or to let you take the lead. Each person needs the grace and the knowledge to know when to step back and when to step forward.

The Divine Partnership
So many males right now are tentative about how to act. The raging feminists in pink pussy hats have done the human race a disservice. At one point things really were toxic, when men felt like they could take whatever they wanted and they did. Now the pendulum has swung the other way where women have become the toxic ones. As for the females who think their rights are being trampled on when a man holds the door open for them, I say, they have a lot to learn.

When the man I am with says, hey do you want me to put your bike together or are you one of those women who feel like they have to do everything for themselves? I say, Here's the screwdriver.

I don't want to be the man. I want to be feminine. But that doesn't mean I let go of the qualities that are the hallmark of manhood, like leadership, logic, and strength. I am secure in those qualities and can draw from them as needed. I am great with a screwdriver but I don't need to use one to show I am capable. Let's all just relax a bit.

Obviously women can be the handy person and men can be the chef, but these sorts of superficial gender roles don't matter. Whether women are more emotional and men are more analytical also doesn't matter. The point is to be with someone who balances you and whom you balance in return. Together you become the embodiment of both the divine masculine and the divine feminine. That is the true divine partnership.

Sacred Sex

Our conceptions have become convoluted as to what constitutes physical intimacy. Everything down is up and everything up is down. Why is sex taboo? Why is it so often presented as simple animalistic gratification? Sex in a loving partnership where you are emotionally connected can be the most glorious, uplifting, transcendent act on earth. It is physically as well as spiritually and emotionally satisfying.

It is not dirty and anything you choose to do, as long as it's consensual and not harming anybody or anything is not dirty or bad.

As for sacred sex, when you move into a truly loving relationship and are with your divine partner, sex sends you to other realms. If you're lucky, you will astral travel. You'll go other places. Sometimes you hallucinate. The best mind expanding drug you can have is sexual union with a divine partner.

Your Divine Partner

Your divine partner is somebody with whom you immediately share connection. This is because they were either sent to you or you've been with them before. You have an ease of being with them, a knowing of each other without having spent much time together as of yet. It's a complimentary way of being that doesn't in any way detract from one other. Instead it supports. Always supports.

Jane: What else?

Lane: Obviously truth, deep truth. This is the basis of intimacy, also chemistry, where there's sexual intensity and connection. You want to physically be with them. They could look like a troll from under the bridge, but to you, they're beautiful, because you see their inner being. To me, my twin flame was physically beautiful, although others didn't think so.

Divine partnership is seeing straight through to each other's inner being, and not just seeing it, but treasuring what you find there. Your sexual attraction never wanes, no matter how old you are. Does their head swivel when a 19 year old with insouciant breasts pops by? Well, if the tongue falls out and the eyes bulge, you've got the wrong guy.

Couples who say they're allowed to look or have sex with partners outside their relationship are not in divine partnerships. If they are, they haven't discovered it yet and are tossing it away.

Jane: So how do you define divine partnership?

Lane: It's an elevation, it's not even needing to speak, but when you do speak, you speak forever. You can sit on a bench and watch clouds and not be bored. You don't want to be with anyone else.

That goes for insouciant breasts or bulging biceps. It's okay to admire beauty, but not to lust after it. If that happens, it's a sign you are in the wrong relationship. Either that, or you need to define how you really, on the most deeply intimate level, feel about each other.

Jane: When you're home alone by yourself, at your ugliest, who is the person that can sit next to you and support you in your journey to be the best version of yourself, especially when you're at your worst? When my partner fails to do something the way I wish it was done, and I want to show him how fabulous I am and how not fabulous he is, that's not a good situation to be creating.

Observe this and then acknowledge it. I didn't like how I showed up that day. I don't like how I felt. You tell him, I don't like the way I treated you, then you admit what your real fear is. Maybe you don't want to be in control of everything, and when he can't do something as well as you, it sends you into fear.

This can launch into a real deep beautiful conversation of vulnerability, which from there leads to a very uplifting conversation of him wanting the best for you and you wanting the best for him. So the divine partner is the person who sits next to you when you are at your absolute worst and still wants the best for you and helps you to get through that and you do exactly the same for them.

Are You With the Right Partner?

Lane: So many people who are evolving are suddenly finding themselves on a different timeline or let's say headspace from their current partner.

Jane: The easy answer to this would be to consciously uncouple and move on. As hard as that might be in a 3D world, it's actually the easy answer.

Lane: But there could be a better answer or a higher answer. Separating doesn't necessarily mean it's the right answer.

Jane: I think it's very important that a higher answer doesn't mean better or right. It just means a different way. What is unconditional love? Can you do it?

Lane: Let's hold on to that for a second. That would be the best outcome. If you have unconditional love for each other and you're prepared to help bring that person with you on your journey.

But what happens if you discover that the person you're with is in essence your handler, or somebody who is dead set on holding you back? He or she may not even realize it. It's them being so mired in a 3D mindset, that you feel there is no other way forward than pulling out. Is it selfish to go onward and to leave, especially when you've pledged a lifetime together?

Jane: I'm not a fan of that lifetime pledge at all. I don't think that we have any right to promise anything of any length to anyone. I think the promise is that we show up and commit to do our best to support each other, to be the best versions of ourselves.

I can promise to love my husband for the rest of my life, and that is absolutely my intention and still is my intention, but I can't control him. What if he turns around tomorrow and says, I never expected this to happen. You know, I love you, but I've met somebody who I just can't stop thinking about. I can't control that. So I don't get to make a promise that I can't necessarily keep.

Lane: Right. And what if he's turned to violence? I mean, am I meant to still love this guy and hang around?

Jane: I think pledge is a program to control and manipulate us.

Lane: To give another twist to that, in coming to terms with leaving my own marriage, because I also thought that when I was marrying, I was pledging for a lifetime, I had no idea that our, let's say, timelines were going to diverge so severely.

When they did, there was no going back. He was on a completely different level, and I'm not saying that in an egotistical way, but he was hell bent on staying in the box he created for himself. There was just no getting around it. The realization I came to over the years since we were together is that we may not have just one partner in this lifetime.

We are evolving so quickly and in such divergent ways. How can one person fulfill you for a full lifetime? I've probably reinvented myself six times over the past 30 years. Probably more. After my marriage, I fell into a twin flame relationship that took me to heaven and hell and back again.

It sped up my evolvement so fast, it took years to break down all I had learned. I'm still breaking it down in some senses.

Jane: I think you better define twin flame. When defining twin flames and differentiating the term from soulmates and sacred partners, I feel like we need to throw all of these labels out and find new terms.

Lane: Yes, but as soon as we find a new term, the Deep State would place a sign on it. For example, there's a show produced by the bad guys about twin flames.

Jane: It's been twisted, just like anything pure has been twisted. They would twist it to make sure that we look like idiots, because we are the most powerful on the planet, and we are the biggest threat to them.

Lane: Not only do they twist it, they use it as a way of blocking the truth. So now, if I as a normal person who hasn't done a lot of deep research, go searching for information on Twin Flames, I'm going to continually get led to the Netflix show, instead of to the real info that I'm looking for.

There's search techniques to get around this, but the average person doesn't know them. This happens time and again when there's an important concept or information out there. They simply block it by putting something else out there using the same terminology.

Jane: They'll twist the meaning, implying there's something dark and sinister about it, and then they will, as you say, block it in search engines, so it becomes suppressed, distorted, and hidden.

Lane: Yes. They will invert and hide it. We need new terms and new ways of looking at things. So we attract and choose partners and there are no mistakes

Jane: Every relationship is divine. And every relationship is with a soulmate.

Lane: I would say every relationship is with someone from your soul group. Every relationship has moments of being a twin flame. Every relationship has moments of being a soul sister or brother.

Jane: We're all soul sisters and brothers, and well said, I agree, that's it.

Lane: I will say that the twin flame term, though we need to get rid of these labels, is not necessarily the relationship that's going to last the longest in your life. The really important aspect to the relationship with this person, is that it is a humongous mirror.

Now, everyone is a mirror because everyone's going to mirror back what's functional and dysfunctional about you. But a twin flame is going to do it in an extreme way, and sometimes in such a fast way that the person could be in and out of your life in a heartbeat, a few years, or maybe it'll last forever.

The traditional explanation of a twin flame is someone with

whom you experience almost instant unexplainable attraction. If it's a love relationship you share immense passion and deep feeling. On the other side of that is great distress, for it's a hugely polar relationship. For mirroring all the good and wonderfulness are dark and difficult times that come with it.

The reason for this is that this individual has been thrown into your path to help you advance quickly, to make things happen at an accelerated rate. It may burn itself out and may not last, but that's not what's important. What is important is taking the ride.

As difficult as it may be, it's important to thank the Universe for the experience.

Jane. When you and I came together, holy moly, we were like opposites of the same coin. We were from opposite sides of the world. We didn't even have to use words.

Jane: That was such a special moment of instant deep knowing of each other. Just more proof of design synchronicity in action. It's also the growing of our ability to connect with our tribe easily and effortlessly.

What I love about this, and a lot of people started to experience this in their own way of by virtual signaling during COVID. You'd go into a supermarket for instance, and you've got 99 percent of the people there masked. Then you turn down an aisle or walk into another shop and there's somebody else who's also unmasked.

You glance at each other and there's a knowing. I was in a bakery in a country town and this guy walked in and took one look at me then walked up and hugged me. I said, oh, hello stranger. And he said, hello family. We had glimpses of it then. Another time I'd be dodging the QR check-in code to get into a shop, and someone else would be doing the same thing, and we'd just share that knowing sideways look.

Lots of people have been experiencing things like this. Sometimes we have the experience of just meeting somebody and then you look into their eyes and there's a knowing. I really appreciate it most when that happens with somebody who, in our 3D societal structure, you would not normally find commonality with, like a middle aged woman and a 20 year old punk rocker covered in tats.

In other words, between those who seem completely opposite to one another physically in age, socioeconomic position. But when your eyes meet, you get that special little nod of acknowledgement from one to the other. You know, you've just crossed paths with another member of our soul family.

Lane: Perhaps the question is, what is a relationship? And what is it that people want from a relationship?

Jane: Being with somebody who isn't growing at the same rate of you may be difficult, but there may be other aspects that you find valuable.

This is where it gets really complex in relationships, and to be able to guide on this is a very individual thing. I guess where I come from in having been a matchmaker, and particularly with people in their 30s, 40s and beyond, most come to me post long term relationship separation. What I saw was an awful lot of people who ended a relationship thinking the grass is greener.

In other words, they thought their happiness was external, not having done the internal work. So we've got two different groups. One group is, have you done the work? If you haven't done the work, then you stay with that person that you're with until you've done the work.

Then you can consciously decide if that person's right for you or not for the next chapter of evolution of your life. But if you have done the work, then you're going to have a different answer.

Lane: What if you can't do the work while you're in that particular situation?

Jane: I think you can do the work wherever you are.

There's always going to be exceptions. That's the problem that we have though, when the majority of people believe that they are the exception, what we've got then is self delusion.

Lane: If you're in a marriage typical of women in a suburban environment, they're comfortable, their husbands are making a decent living, they have a nice house, they have a social network, their kids are in good schools, they're reasonably happy, they go out, have nice clothes. But there is something lacking at the core of their existence.

They can't put their finger on it because they haven't embarked on the soul work some have done. Sometimes, it isn't until you find solitude when you are on your own that you can truly start a new level of inner work.

Jane: I love that, but I don't necessarily think it's always true. I'm in a long term relationship and yet I don't think I could have done any deeper work than I have done. I get what you're saying though. It's the person who's cruising life. They may want to do it, but in reality they'd rather go to the golf course or the book club. That's spiritual bypassing. It's no different to the shopaholic, the workaholic, the alcoholic. It doesn't matter what *aholic*, the person is numbing out from life.

There will be those reading this book who have people they care for and love deeply who fall into this category, and it's a case of letting them be. At some point for the majority, something will happen. There will be a crisis that will occur, a trauma perhaps. Not that I'm wishing this for anyone. It could be the loss of someone. It could be an illness. It could be a sudden bankruptcy in the family, something unexpected that shocks them. As they try to reconcile how that occurs, that's the entry point and their self development will open up.

When Structures Break Down

When I left my marriage, I did not realize I was leaving the family unit and an entire social circle and all my best friends and everybody else I was acquainted with. Because everything was free flowing. I didn't have a plan. Afterwards I went through multiple holidays alone. Christmas traditions had been important to me, but I lost them, and the joy in them. New Year's Eve? It was important for me to kiss the man I loved at midnight. I mean, I'm a New York City girl, so being alone at this time was very painful.

Yet while it was incredibly sad it also was empowering. You learn a few things like how to not put importance on holidays. It's not about the holidays. You learn to find the joy in the family whenever gatherings occur. If it's no longer got a Christmas stamp on it, that's okay. Things change. Some might fill the void with work, and at times I fell into that.

People fear going into the nothingness. But as the structures beneath our feet, every last one, crumbles, what is not left is a void, but yourself. There you find yourself.

There is a reason for the removal of that most beloved structure of all, the connection to our families during holiday time.

As that is taken from us we cannot let it bring us down, however we fill it. I say, don't worry about filling it in the beginning. The growth will come, as long as you let it.

Chapter 6: Creating a Magic Shift

I have a theory. I think that we are concentrating better, going deeper, and as individuals, channeling more than ever before. The switch from one energy zone to another is not always easy to navigate, and it sometimes happens in the blink of an eye. We're traveling in different energy systems and almost entirely using our right brains at these times. It's not that you don't have the bandwidth, you simply aren't able to go into that left brain at these moments. Instead of being hard on yourself when you're suddenly unable to do easy math, for example, keep this in mind. You are connecting on deeper, more esoteric levels than you realize.

We're pulling things out we haven't done before, going places beyond our conscious reality. Personally I'm keeping things free flowing, until everything lands where it lands.

You might find this book unusual in that we have not yet gone over the Laws of the Universe. Like the energy around us at this time, this book is in a free flow meant to address where we are on multiple levels at once.

Jane: The reason that you didn't want to go over the Laws of the Universe or anything like that is you didn't want to be influenced by outside thought.

Lane: A lot of what is out there is discordant with me. I want to keep this book strictly between me and Source, if that can be done. When I read other contemporary material, it's not so much to derive information as it is to figure out a resonant way to address something. Usually one word or passage acts as a springboard to an outpouring of thought.

When I read somebody from ancient times, who writes in a prose that's hard to understand, there's an interpretation level that's difficult to bridge. Yet the essence of what he was saying is profound.

I would never take what anyone says verbatim because all of the information, even Edgar Cayce and Paramahansa Yogananda who's work was groundbreaking and which defined new levels of spirituality, relay material that does not always work with the times. Sometimes human advancement takes a different trajectory. We've got core concepts, but human advancement since their material was written calls for different input.

Magic Shift Tool 1: Your Emotional Barometer

Some of their work is so brilliant it defies explanation, like the explanation Edgar Cayce shares for ego. Cayce said, "ego is not the enemy of self knowledge. It is the path to it." Then he says, "for it is in the application, not the knowledge that the truth becomes part of thee."

That statement defines our core path as human beings. In other words, by working through the reasons behind human ego, we find the way to self knowledge and enlightenment.

I personally find it difficult to use workbooks and worksheets and to follow plans and steps. I prefer to incorporate a way of thinking into my being which then becomes actionable, which is the primary reason this book is written the way it is.

When faced with workbooks and lesson plans, I glaze over. This is not to say that they don't provide great assistance to those who can utilize them. Instead I operate off my emotional barometer.

Jane: Would I be right in saying that when you're reading books by other authors, you're using them as a scanning mechanism to determine what is in alignment?

Lane: Yes, and it's actually a validation either way.

Jane: How can people learn to connect to their emotions and use this barometer, this scanning?

Lane: To know what is true for them versus what is a trigger for them versus what is relevant for them.

This is part of the way of thinking I'm talking about. In the steps to perception, how you are being indoctrinated, what is real and what is not, it comes down to what I call empirical truth. You've got to break everything down to what is true. Notice I did not say factual because facts are easily skewed.

When you break things down, you will realize there's really only a few things you can hold onto as absolutely true.

Jane: Some will say that includes fear.

Lane: Fear is imposed. It's not an empirical truth. Being in fear is an invitation to explore. As in, what's your trigger? What is your unhealed self? It's just like following ego, as Cayce said.

It's very simple. Follow ego and fear to their source and you have the blueprint for self enlightenment. If you strip away everything false, you come down to empirical truth. Truth about you, truth about the world. Fear is imposed for the most part. Now, we're not talking fight or flight. There is a bear chasing you in the woods, you run. That's different.

Fear in general is imposed. It's not real. When you strip away fear and all these false histories and this bogus government system and man made diseases, when you strip away religion and educational systems, when you strip it all down, what is real?

I'll tell you what. For me, it's God, personal integrity—or as some would say authenticity—and unconditional love. That's it. You just can't destroy any of those three. Look at the mother whose child has been killed on the battlefield. She's still able to love the person who shot her child.

That's called unconditional love. It's very hard to do, but it can be done. Going back to our scanning mechanism and what is in alignment and what isn't, you have to first go back to the starting place. You need the baseline. What's the baseline?

If it's not resonating, if it's not in love or in alignment with Source, which are basically the same things, you have to examine it. If there is no real answer there at this time, yet seems to have truth in it, you hold it in abeyance.

In other words, you hold it as a possibility until it's either confirmed or refuted.

Jane: I think this is a very important technique to talk about. If there is a potential grain of truth in it, if you get a bit of a nod of, *hmm, that's a possibility*, you hold it for further examination. I think that is a wonderful gift which we must highlight.

If people were to add that one tool, their world would change immediately.

Lane: Sometimes it's hard to figure out. We have to go back to discernment, which is a practice. Those in this ascension truth movement have had the benefit of years of scanning alleged truth tellers until we got so good at it, we could tell who was lying, who was telling partial truths, and who was being paid by the cabal, ten seconds into a video. But that came after years of work. For others now coming into this, the process is sped up.

Magic Shift Tool 2: The Love Principle

There is not always a right or wrong answer, and just because somebody is telling a mistruth doesn't mean that their heart is in the wrong place. You have to read energy. That sounds daunting, but in reality reading energy is something we actually all do.

Normal people do it every day. You can tell when somebody's negative or somebody's positive, but then you dig even deeper to understand where are they coming from. Why are they saying that particular thing? This ties into unconditional love. Love for your fellow humans, I mean. I don't mean just giving food to people who are homeless and working in soup kitchens or buying Christmas presents for the poor. While that's lovely, that's not necessarily true love for humanity. You need to love everyone, even the alleged bad guys.

You have to understand that every single person has a story. Should they be forgiven? Should they be allowed to be let loose and to commit crimes on innocents? No, of course not.

Notice I said person, or in other words, humans. There are entities who do not belong in that classification. The evils they perpetrate are beyond human comprehension. They do not belong on this planet and should be sent back to wherever they came from.

Understanding other humans can bring you to a point of unconditional love. If you have unconditional love in your heart, you can more easily discern because you're not laying blame. You're not judging. Unconditional love and not judging go hand in hand.

You don't have to work on judgment if you work on love because the judgment falls away.

You may still experience triggers, but that's because we're works in progress. Always. But the practice of unconditional love accelerates our growth process tenfold.

Magic Shift Tool 3: Past Life Memories

I think past life regressions are really interesting tools. You told me that you discovered you were not as a good person back in the Atlantean days.

Jane: It always makes me laugh when people play around with past lives and say, Oh, I was a queen or a king at such and such a time.

Lane: There certainly are a lot of Cleopatras and King Arthurs running around.

Jane: What about the lifetime where you were the murderer or the rapist? I remember one where I was in charge of men that were placed in dungeons, where I abused them pretty badly.

Lane: We have all had what could be conceived as bad, as well as good, or more moral, or let's say normal incarnations. We are collectively on the path of growing and learning.

Jane: In one of the regressions, I remember looking into the eyes of a man that I despised because he never reacted to my abuse. He just took it on board. He was full of grace and inner peace. I remember the moment when I looked into his eyes and saw love because he knew I was just playing a role. I was experiencing a particular way of being for my own soul growth.

I'll never forget those eyes. It was very powerful. And I remember thinking, I want to be like him. My role model came to me from the victim I was abusing.

Lane: Those lifetimes where you've not been the great person are very interesting to explore. There's a certain humility involved in uncovering times when you are not exhibiting the best of qualities.

Jane: Atlantis was not one that I was very proud of.

Lane: But you are unique to uncovering a past life where you were perpetrating evil. Usually we're very protected against uncovering those lifetimes.

It may wound us deeply to learn that we hurt other people in previous incarnations. I've had at least one experience where I know I was doing things that were very bad. I did a particular regression years ago because I wanted to know what was going on between myself and a family member. I think selective past life memory is a self protection device.

At least for me it was.

Jane: I agree with that. There was a reason that I had to uncover this lifetime in Atlantis. I was one of three men who were leading the destruction of the Lemurians because in that lifetime I considered those people to be insipid, pathetic, and insignificant. Boring, delusional, uninteresting. I used terms that we would hear now from someone like Klaus Schwab.

Lane: Useless eaters.

Jane: Yes, that was exactly how I saw the Lemurians in that lifetime. So I understand at a different level, therefore, where the World Economic Forum puppets are coming from. Now, do I agree with them in this lifetime? Not at all. I've signed up to fight the good fight against them.

Lane: That's amazing. I can remember two lifetimes during that period. One, I was a scientist and I did not know anything beyond my laboratory. I did not know how my work was being used to hurt others. I didn't care. No, it's more that I didn't care to know. You've got your face in a microscope or whatever the mechanics were, and you don't see anything beyond that. It was selective myopia.

The other lifetime I remember in Lemuria allows me to see how it all works, meaning where humanity is progressing. I can feel our new utopia.

This is part of the plan for humanity given by the Arcturians, which I'll be sharing with those who want it. But back to your Atlantis lifetime. Basically, you destroyed my people.

Jane: Uh, yes. When I realized that, I also realized that my world in this lifetime is full of those beautiful people. I knew that my ego in this lifetime had the power to destroy every single relationship I had. Delving into this and the understanding I gained, I chose to use the emotional scanner technique. I did the scans to clear and then I would go through triggering content deliberately to test how I'm doing, healing this negative part of me, this power hungry greed that I had.

I don't have it now, but it took me a good 10 years to fully remove it.

Lane: The thing to remember is that you have control over the recall of past lives and also their residual effects. Feeling your way through all of it will help you heal in this lifetime, as well as prevent possibly damaging actions on your part now.

Magic Shift Tool 4: Inner Scanner Test

Jane: I was raised in a family where I was to do my best to play in the elitist system and I loved it. I was drawn to celebrities. I was drawn to fame and fortune. Actually, fame and fortune was the by product. What I actually wanted was the power. I knew this was very dangerous and I did the work on this, a great deal of inner work with many amazing therapists and methods.

This went on until I got to a point where I completely trusted myself. And then along came COVID and the inner scanner tests were applied. I confirmed I wasn't for sale and I didn't go down the power path. I feel like I'm rock solid and stable now, but it did take a lot of work. Through all of that, I learned about the indoctrination.

I learned about discernment. I learned about judgment. I learned about love. I learned about finessing the scanning ability. It's a commitment to consistently scan. Like now, for example, I'm looking for what's still triggering me. I'll jump onto our newsfeed and I'll scan everything to see what I've not dealt with yet. What I get triggered by is what I've got to deal with now.

Lane: There is a fine line between being triggered and disgusted.

Jane: Oh yes, trigger will put me in fear.

Lane: That's exactly right. A trigger will generate a debilitating involuntary reaction.

Jane: It will disempower me versus disgust me. So disempowerment is very different. Fear is something I've got to deal with versus *I can't believe those bastards think they're going to roll this out. I can't wait to watch the pushback.*

Lane: The reason I bring up disgust is that because it is my reaction when something is out of resonance. In other words, there is something wrong. I had to learn to respect this reaction because at first I mistook it for being triggered. Now I know it's part of my scan.

Jane: The scanning is interesting to me, and it's also a scan of knowledge, because they've created the matrix in such an intricate web. I think it will probably take the rest of this lifetime for me to really understand just how brilliant a job they've done.

Magic Shift Tool 5: Swap this for Blind Faith

I don't believe in faith for faith's sake. I live in Christ Consciousness and I have belief in a Higher Power. I have faith because Source, or my guides, are going to flag the situation if I'm doing something that's not going to end well, or if it's not on my soul's path to experience. If I'm not supposed to die that day, they're going to pull me out of the ocean during a sudden rip tide, which happened to me this summer. I have an understanding that they will protect me, and that to me is faith. Obviously I'm not going to go jump off a cliff and see if they're going to save me, but if I accidentally tripped and tumbled down an embankment of steel and broken concrete, which happened to me in Albania, I know they will keep me from doing any severe damage, particularly as I asked for their help while going down.

There's got to be an understanding that you have other forces at play who are watching over you. This is generally true unless you're acting against the laws of karma, or in other words, what you sow you reap. If that is this case, all bets are off. If you're in your heart space and doing everything you can to be in alignment with Source and all that is good, then your guides and angels will help if you ask them. This doesn't mean you can't enjoy yourself, as long as it doesn't involve harming others. But you do need to stay in alignment with Source.

Once you're in alignment, then you've got to trust that your guides and whatever benevolent spirits might working with you, are walking beside you.

Jane:. Would you like to talk more about faith?

Lane: I think this is a conclusion gathered from the evidence that you are protected, and a belief in a divinity. It's not an imposed belief because you went to a religious service and were told how it goes. It's from lived experience.

Magic Shift Tool 6: Checking In

I have a secret super power in the form of my mom, who has been so on it, so connected, that it made it easy to just ask her to check in on things for me.

If I was set to travel during the pandemic for instance, I'd say, *Ma, can I really go at this time?* And she'd check and say, *You'll be fine. It would be great if you didn't have to do it during mercury retrograde, but you'll be fine.*

While I still check in with her from time to time, I also do it myself. This is merely asking and checking the response. If you don't get a solid feeling one way or another, keep alert for signs. If things start to go wrong, such as your flights get switched or a meeting got cancelled, double check: should you really be going at this time?

Say you have a traffic jam and miss your plane. What's the real reason you just missed that flight? When I missed my connecting flight to to Rome, yes, it was a huge pain and I lost a whole day and had to stay in a hotel, not knowing anyone. I just accepted there was a reason for that, one I may never know.

Magic Shift Tool 7: Outsmart Karma

Karma is tricky. Karma is wonderful. I just don't like to experience it.

Jane: So what do you do about that?

Lane: You learn your lessons quickly and effectively and don't do it again. Karma can be lessened and even eliminated. As I mentioned earlier, there's a theory I've been working on my entire life.

Jane: Can you eliminate harsh karmic lessons if you have learnt your lesson on the spot?

Lane: Yes, and part two of that would be thanking the Universe for that experience, and I mean it. Don't just say, Oh yeah, thanks.

No, it's thank you for that enlightening situation because now I know not to do that again. And you need to feel the gratitude and in going even further to love the experience as Nietzsche said.

Jane: When we find the gift in every experience, we don't need to repeat the experience. My question to someone would be, what is it that you now know about yourself that you didn't know about yourself prior to this experience?

As you identify what that is, whether it's positive or negative, you become conscious of it instead of it being a subconscious reaction.

Lane: We bring it to the conscious. We bring it to the light. Therefore, there is no need for that to be repeated.

Jane: And that's what you've been saying, that the karma will dissipate.

Lane: It's a lifetime of putting the pieces together. I made a covenant with God a long time ago. I was very young and I said, God, I don't want karma. Thank you. I will learn my lessons on the spot. Thank you so much. Because I don't want bad experiences. So I made a covenant then and I've probably done that on a million other levels without even thinking. It's part of my being. I just make a little deal with my guides.

Magic Shift Tool 8: Memories, Covenants and Contracts

Jane: Let's talk about covenants because I don't think people do what you do at all.

Lane: All right. I eradicated any soul contracts because I feel it is grossly wrong for us not to remember what we have contracted to before commencing our current lives.

I know this flies in the face of a lot of, let's say spiritual type thinking, but this unfairness pertains to recalling past lives as well. This lack of memory feels like an artificial construct that the bad side has concocted. They've put a veil up. Many people maintain that the veil of forgetfulness is there for our protection, and while that's probably true to some degree, I feel we should be able to access those lives and information more readily than we can right now.

Recall is harder than it should be.

Jane: I do think that the veil has been hijacked and the dumbing down of the race has continued for a very long time as they've got more and more complex in their matrix and manipulation of the veil. I 100% agree that we should be remembering our past lives to have new experiences.

Lane: To understand and explore just a handful of past lives took a lot of money and work. At one point, I did two years of regressions for a difficult relationship that I needed to explore in order to understand. I was having a very hard time comprehending why I was with this abusive personality. I loved him and he loved me, but it was like fire and water.

So, I went through these sessions extracting the information through emotional resonance, if you will, gaining bits and pieces at a time. The work involved in pulling out these memories is immensely difficult, yet the information is enlightening. When you gain insight into your past lives, your level of understanding in this life grows in proportion.

The memories are not going to cure all your problems, but you can understand things much better and find a pathway through them. This pathway brings you back to love, compassion, empathy, all of those things. I also realized that I had in some form contracted with this person, a contract I then broke.

Jane: So at this point you renegotiated soul contracts and your covenants?

Lane: I did renegotiate them. That's why I brought up past lives. I think it's a false construct that we do not remember them except in very isolated incidents. I call BS on that one.

Jane: Me too.

Lane: The other thing I call BS on is not knowing what our soul contracts say. If I signed anything or agreed to anything, I deserve to know it consciously in this lifetime.

I need to know what I agreed to. So what I did was say loudly and with force, I refute and negate any and all soul contracts that I have ever entered into. They are worthless. They don't exist. They're gone. Something to that effect. I say that periodically, but I also say this, God, whatever you want me to do, I will do, or whatever I need to do and to stay in alignment with you, Source, I will do, but I just need to consciously know.

Magic Shift Tool 9: Isolating Your Purpose

What I mean by knowing is the intuitive sense that you're on the correct path and that you're doing what you, to the best of your knowledge, think you should be doing. It is helpful to find your true purpose on the planet.

Jane: And how do you do that?

Lane: Go back to when you were a very young child and try to recall what your dreams were.

What did you want to do? Then and now, what makes your soul sing? Instead of going to your drudge job every day, what would set your passion on fire? What brings you joy and fulfillment? Finding that is your pathway to resonance with Source. For me, it started with creativity. I never for a second let go of any of my dreams, not one of them.

Jane: What were your dreams when you were young?

Lane: This may sound egotistical, but this became my guiding rule. I knew from a very young age that I was here to do something important. I could feel it at times. It was ephemeral. Just beyond my reach, something very large that I could barely perceive. It's a feeling that's recurred many times over my life.

Now, between you, me, and the readers of this book, my mom always said, oh, you're such royalty, load the dishwasher. And I'd think, yes, I am royalty, and I shouldn't have to do dishes. That didn't work very well.

Now the Arcturians call me their queen. I don't say that to make myself sound grander than I am. Maybe they have many queens. Maybe it's a term of respect for them. I've had plenty of lifetimes of drudgery, and this lifetime has had its share of experiences which have been challenging, if not eye opening and transportive.

But going back to my passions, they've always centered on creativity, and I've never changed that. I can envision new worlds. I can write a business plan that defies conventions. I can create beauty from whatever is on hand, whether it's a pile of twigs, someone's life story, or leftovers in the fridge.

There has always been art, music, and writing for me. At one point, I wanted to be an actress. When I became a New York City talent agent, however, I said, oh my dear God, this is how it works? No, thank you. So from there, I went into playwriting and directing, and that's where I found a path. I could orchestrate the whole scenario with input from collaborators in a way I found both challenging and fulfilling.

Then I worked with children, which opened up another level. When I say I never left my dreams, I mean they evolved into a throughline that I've held on to. The pathway is creativity. This is not isolated to me. Creativity is universal, and it will connect you to the divine if you let it. The task is to find what's creative in your soul, and I assure you, it's there.

Chapter 7: The Dimensional Spectrum

You've no doubt heard a lot of the "dimensions" from the woo woo spiritual community, of which I suppose I'm a member. However I like staying grounded with explanations that I can understand and terminology that doesn't need an interpreter.

3D, 4D and 5D

You might have heard of the third dimension, the fourth dimension, and the fifth dimension. Although the dimensions go much higher, these are the three we are most concerned with right now. I refer to 3D a lot. That's third dimension. To me it's a shorthand way of speaking. I try not to label or to put people down, but when I use the word 3D, it refers to a certain mindset.

The 3D mindset in general terms means that they are still watching mainstream television, being generally brainwashed by media, politicians, big Pharma and the like, while not admitting to indoctrinated thought or choosing to see past it. They buy into dogma. They take the word of "authorities" as truth. They believe in the system. They have not seen into the truth of things, nor do they wish to see further than their insulated lives. They're what is considered normal.

Normal people watch baseball games, find only minor problems with the school system, and take the kids to sports and dance lessons and conduct regular medical check ups where they are put on a vaccine schedule. They watch TV shows after work and listen to news in the car. They get the Disney channel and go to church, synagogue or the mosque. There is nothing wrong with any of this on the face of it. We all do these things to some extent. The problem is not seeing past the false nature of things. We are living in an illusion and that includes all of the above. Some say that we are living in a matrix, and all you need to do to get out of it is to see it.

Third dimension moves into the fourth dimension, which is a little less dense, a little more enlightened. But this is also where the negative dwells: the evil reptiles and Dracos, and other negative entities. Navigating this level is a process of evolvement, where you meet your innermost demons and work through the trauma of the past. It is a rite of passage, or so it is said.

I call BS once again, and personally decided to skip the fourth dimension. I didn't want any part of that, if the above was true. I decided to work out my inner demons in a state of full light, if you will. In other words I was not intending on avoiding the inner work, but I would do it as I do everything, steadily, as I evolve. If there is one theme to this book it is to not take anyone's word as absolute. I know too many people who wrangle with the darkness. They fall into drugs or alcohol or self pity. This may very well be a necessary rite of passage for some. I personally choose not to go there.

Many of us are part of the fifth dimension now, which is a fully awake and aware, unconditionally loving state of being. We can easily detect energetic vibrations. We hear and see things that other people don't perceive. I get a sense of smell, which pops up out of nowhere when I'm tapping into the energy of a place or event. This phenomenon is weird and interesting. It first happened while I was browsing real estate listings. I started smelling the odors of places I was looking at. All I can say is I moved on from those listings quickly.

5D is a different way of being and a different energy. It's clean and beautiful and free. The things that chain other people are not part of your reality. It's perceiving things in five dimensions instead of three. You are not in any boxes here. You have a sense of freedom that others can barely understand. If you are still holding onto false dogmas or structures, you are learning to identify and purge them on the way to full-on empirical truth and personal authenticity. There are downfalls, of course. You don't have as many people to relate to. You can't take idle chit chat. You may no longer find the same pleasure in watching sports or movies. Yet you appreciate when work is elevated, no matter the field of endeavor.

In so many respects 5D is way, way better. I'm looking forward to the day when more people climb on board.

Navigating the Dimensions

Jane: I think we're fully in the fourth dimension demonic war, but I feel like I can just banish the interference and they don't get to Wi Fi me. I'm sure we've all got the hardware in us regardless of whether we've been vaxxed or not.

Lane: Yeah, as far as I'm concerned, I left 3D a long time ago and went right to 5D. It's not egotistical, it's not a popular theory, it's just the way it is. I skipped over 4D because I don't acknowledge it. If people want to fight demons, that's their business. This includes fallout from the VAX, including 5G and graphene, which they're using to control people.

We're in this situation where the earth is battling it out, and we need all our resources, which is why I choose not to weaken mine.

Jane: So what are we supposed to be doing? I think we know, but how do we navigate being in 5D, helping out, and yet not letting it affect us?

Lane: I think we're doing pretty well, all things considered, but it is a strange place to be.

Every single spokesperson that I give any credence to whatsoever, who is a seer or intel provider of some sort, I already know what they're going to say before they say it. It's not BS, because they're doing their darndest to get the word out, but I've been there and done that.

That's how I feel about most everything that's being said out there right now. What is interesting, however, is that we're seeing people fight back against the division. That's the light side winning. We're seeing people say that all people are suffering. It's not about one group or another. In the Israeli Palestine situation, we've been inundated with talking heads telling us what to think or what side to be on.

This state we are in is not about one person over the other or one side over the other. This is about fairness and liberation for humanity. If we can't get this right, we're not going to move forward. This gathering of forces against oppression is critical right now. I can see it happening.

Jane: I agree. I said to somebody recently who was questioning the yes, no vote, which we had here in Australia with the Indigenous being recognized in the constitution. I said, we have to learn to get along. Until we can do that, the rest of it is just smoke and mirrors. I love that we're seeing people step up.

There was a cute little meme that popped up the other day that said, I'm not pro Russia, I'm not pro Ukraine, I'm not pro Israel, I'm not pro Vaxx, I'm not pro Anti, and listed all of the different divisions ending with I'm pro people. I think that articulates what you're saying in a different way.

Moving Past 4D

Jane: I'm fascinated that you jumped 4D.

Lane: My mom and I have this perpetual back and forth on whether or not I skipped 4D, and I'm maintaining that I did.

She says, but everyone has to go through it, it's part of the process. And I say, who said it's part of the process? Why does it have to be part of the process? Who said we have to go through the dark side of existence on this planet? I've already been through the dark night of the soul, I don't need more of that stuff.

But here's what put it over the top for me. My significant

other at the time, the twin flame I've talked about, would fight battles in 4D at night in a sleep state. He told me some of what went down. It's scary, dark stuff. He'd awaken with cuts and bruises on his body. That was the death knell for me.

I said, I am simply going to be my 5D self, hopefully ascending further than that. By the 5D self meaning not judgmental. It's perpetually moving forward. It's in an unconditional love space. Sometimes there's a little slip up. It's hard for us humans. Sometimes we get triggered and that's just as we've said, putting a target on a wound saying, Oh, what's that? Better heal this trigger.

Jane: I remember when I was on a zoom with these allegedly beautiful humanitarians. One of the men said, when we talk to XYZ person, we need to be speaking in 3D language. I thought to myself, you patronizing sod. That statement is contradictory to what I believe 5D is, and you've just outed yourself. That kind of talk is a sure tip off that you've got a lot of healing to still do.

Lane: That's so true. I think that spiritual elitism is alive and thriving with 5D people perceiving themselves as superior to others. This superiority has to go. The simple act of thinking you're better means you've not ascended to a higher level.

I dislike using the term 5D, but to me it is very handy because it describes what I want to say efficiently. This is why I grasped onto it. In general, I don't like labels, and elitism in its many forms is something that curdles my blood and always has.

Dimensions Roadblock: The Egoic Mind

I have been in those "elite" circles, and I've been in the lowest of the low circles, and I see them all as equals. The exception is the ones who are harming others. There is so much bad that they do, but the smallest example is how they gobble up the best land areas and then block them off. Bill Gates has gathered up millions of acres of farmland and the Bush family has bought up all the water. At the shorelines riffraff like the rest of us can't get to the beaches because they have all the best oceanfront with no access. That is why I really love the town I'm in right now, because they have free beach access on every block. I've been up and down America's coasts and this is unusual. In the most populated areas you can't get on the beaches except at defined spots because there's multi million dollar homes commanding the space. If you drive through certain sections of Florida, for instance, you'll find it dotted with manicured golf courses and ridiculous displays of opulence. This is exclusive to the filthy rich. It's not pretty or beautiful, and it's out of harmony with nature. It is an ostentatious testament to wealth.

Sustainable architecture that is beautiful, blending in with its natural surroundings would be ideal, but is not always attainable. Gaudy for gaudy's sake is cold and dark. Elitism and its trappings is antithetical to ascendance, and is bound to an earthly density. If you go back to the beginning ages of when we came to this planet, we humans became trapped in the densities. For a long time I pondered what density was, and that meant the 3D construct.

This is the density of being mired in the physical. This includes sex for sex sake. Using people. Gaining wealth and status on the backs of others. Gluttony. Reliance on substances. Clinging to the darker aspects of one's personality, such as victimhood, fury, and aggression.

In that construct, we also have tendencies like following the leader and letting somebody else tell you what to do. There is a lack of conscious understanding of what being on this planet together means. Yet somehow we've got to make this work.

3D consciousness is the egoic mind. Here's another term that's been highly overused: service to self. Every action has to be examined as to whether or not it is serving your own ego. Every single thing you do and say, every thought that comes into your head, must be examined to isolate where it is it coming from and why. That's dissolving the egoic mind or ego.

Drama and always being in a crisis is narcissism, of course. These things are self-focused. Instead, get into a conversation with somebody and let the other person speak.

Jane: That's a great exercise.

Lane: And don't say anything. Just give that person your support and what they need from you at that moment, which might be just recognition or the acknowledgement that what they have to say is important. That's service to somebody else as opposed to your egoic mind barging into the conversation and saying *Yeah? I did that 20 years ago. I already knew that.* That's service to self. It may seem to be a subtle difference, but it's very real.

A Dimensional Test

How can you not feel for both the Palestinians and Jews? Why would you pick a side? Both sides are suffering. Why not practice love for all of them and send that energy out to the Universe? Send it out to them and try to help move us out of this light against dark war and forward into unity consciousness. That's another couple of buzzwords, but it's truth, unity consciousness is where we should be headed. This links back to the egoic or the 3D mind.

We've got to realize that a lot of our ego stuff comes from feeling unworthy, lack of self love and the constant need for others to recognize your worth. I think we all know by now, or at least we should, that that kind of recognition needs to come from the self. It doesn't come from the outside.

Outside recognition is hollow, useless, and it's in service to someone else's self. They are giving you acknowledgement because it serves them in that moment. Why would you give outside recognition any credence? Why would that make you feel better? Instead, feel good about your own self and others will follow. They will love and appreciate you because of the way you make them feel.

Love your own self, and love others just as much, if that's possible. At least try to. This is the surest path to 5D.

Jane: I don't know how easy that is. It's difficult for some.

Lane: If you had no food except one loaf of bread, would you give it to somebody on the street? Or would you instead keep it for yourself and your dog and maybe your neighbor?

Jane: That's a toughie. I know people do it and I admire those who can really put others before themselves.

But I think in that situation, I'm going to put my hand out and say, no, I'm feeding my children and animals first.

Lane: I don't disagree. I'm certainly not at the point of saying I've got a loaf of bread left and I'll give it to somebody on the street and that's all I've got and I don't know where the next one's coming from.

It's a really good test though. I also have another test of generosity. If you commit an act of kindness, whether it's leaving a bag of groceries on your neighbor's doorstep or some other random act, can you do it and not tell anyone?

Jane: If the majority of the world chose to do random acts of kindness tomorrow, and they told everybody about it, it's actually going to create a really good movement in a really good energetic way.

I'd be happy for it, but I do understand the ability to be able to gift without telling anyone is a great spiritual growth.

Lane: Yes, so we are talking about 3D to 5D. Maybe it's a bad test. The 3D person can do that random act and spread love, and that's beautiful motivation and encouragement for others. The 5D person would do it and not tell anyone because it's not about receiving anything back or others saying, Oh my gosh, you're such a good person.

Instead, they would hand the person on the street the bread, give them some money and then tell the world they observed someone else doing it. That's how you accomplish both at one time.

Chapter 8: Jumping Dimensions

Here are some tools to navigate the dimensions and to rise into your highest levels of joy.

Jumping Dimensions Tool 1: Stay In Sync

Passion, joy, and creativity are in sync with godliness. Tapping into these things allows us to become Creators of our own worlds. Maybe you do toenail design and create beautiful patterns. Maybe you are a rock collector and you hone rocks into beautiful shiny stones. Pursuing things that are creative pushes you into a Creator mindset and takes you out of your egoic mind. In the pure act of creating something beautiful or intriguing you're finding a new way to communicate, in whatever form your creativity comes in.

A lot of people think they are not creative individuals and have not fully tapped into this potential. They think, *oh, I stink at art*. No, you are creative. Your true self is creative. Get rid of those blockages that are saying you're not, and forget the second grade teacher who made you feel you stunk at drawing trees.

You need to work through all that's keeping you down in 3D density, that makes you feel incapable. Look for what intrigues you. Ascertain your passions. Passion, a rise in vibration and creativity go hand in hand.

Jumping Dimensions Tool 2: Swap this for Apathy

Who gave anyone the right to stand by and live in a happy little bubble while letting others do the work of pushing humanity forward? It's not right to let 2 percent of the people do 98 percent of the work, and this will come back to you if you don't change it.

I don't mean buying Girl Scout cookies, or purchasing a table at a philanthropic event where most of the money goes to overhead. Even feeding the poor, although it is excellent, is not what I'm referring to here either. What is called for here is to be perceptive and to speak that truth. This is called authenticity.

A lack of authenticity weighs you down and keeps you from becoming who you really are. It doesn't necessarily come immediately. The more you act in integrity to your true self, standing firmly in your own shoes and unapologetic of who you are, and uniformly acting with kindness, courage, conviction and compassion, the stronger and more developed you become. Then the faster you'll move into a 5D.

To put it in other terms, 5D is a knowing. It's a oneness with the Creator and the highest energy in this Universe. It's oneness with goodness and where proactive action is not something you have to contemplate because you embody it.

5D is not being bogged down by fear and the petty BS that others are consumed with every moment of every day. It is being 100% authentic to your best, truest self.

Jumping Dimensions Tool: 3 Eradicate Ego

I have an excellent tool for ego that I haven't yet discussed. It's works beautifully, like magic. What is it?

Take the word "I" out of your vocabulary.

Yes, that's right. Try it for one day. Every time you are about to say "I" substitute "we." Believe me, it works. Things change in a matter of hours. As you drop "I" from your vocabulary you will literally feel yourself floating into the upper dimensions.

You can get out of the egoic mind in 24 hours. Simply put this into action. It's like giving up sugar. If you give up sugar for three days, you can get out of your system and you'll never crave it again. That is, until you eat it again, in which case you'll start craving it again. But you'll find it's a quick turnaround.

Don't use the word "I" ever. You'll learn it really doesn't need to be said.

Those of you reading this book are probably saying but, *Hey, wait a minute. You're using "I" right now.* Sometimes using "I" serves a purpose, such as in relaying personal experiences in the hope they will help your readers. But when speaking to groups or in one-on-one conversations I use "we."

Jumping Dimensions Tool 4: Identify Your Real Goal

When doing good work, others say, *that's creating really good karma for you.* And I will respond, *That's great, how nice. But I'm not doing it for good karma.*

I'm doing it because that person needs attention at that moment or the world needs to be told the truth about something. That's all. I do it because there's a need for it.

Jane: I wonder if that's just something ingrained.

Lane: I don't know where that comes from exactly. It just needs to be done so you do it. You're not doing it for good karma or any kind of reward.

Jane: The vast majority of people, in my opinion, don't do that. They've got to learn these things. They've got to learn because the childhood trauma happens so young that they move into a defensive subconscious fear based behavior, whereas you skipped that through your very different upbringing.

Lane: My mom had on the wall in the bathroom the saying from Jesus, *do unto others as you would have others do unto you.* That was my parents' answer to virtually everything. To me, it all goes back to do unto others. That's why I do it, because that's how I would want to be treated. Now it's just a matter of habit.

Jumping Dimensions Tool 5: Release Trauma Consciousness

We need to lift out of the consciousness of trauma. Trauma attachment keeps us anchored in this density, or this reality, if you will. That's what 3D is, a reality. It's not my reality, not one

I choose and which no one should choose, in my opinion. We're not talking here about severe trauma that needs years of intense work to heal, but rather giving in to trauma as an excuse, as in: *oh, I was so wounded as a child. That's why I am eating this ice cream or hitting you with this hammer.* I've got news for you. Everyone has been traumatized on one level or another. Maybe not to the same degree you were or in the same manner, but you were put into this life before birth to experience and overcome. Which is it going to be? Are you going to succumb to trauma?

Purging it may be a difficult task, but you're going to have to fight through and heal it. Otherwise you wouldn't be given the gift of being on this planet. I don't believe the Creator gives us any challenge we can't rise above.

Jumping Dimensions Tool 6: Don't Buy Into Separatist Thought

Thinking you know better is part of separatism. As in, *I'm better than them. I studied this and they didn't. They have no idea what they're talking about.* Let me tell you something. The more you know, the less you know.

The saying might also be, *the more you know, the less you should say because you've still got a lot to learn.*

Separatist thinking is hugely 3D. LGBTQT is a big test to see are we going to unite or if we are going to separate. The same with ANTIFA. We've got to have sympathy for each other. That goes for all sides. It's wrong to be foisting belief systems on others, particularly on impressionable children. That needs to be fought against and stopped. The people who are perpetuating it are very often heavily programmed themselves and do not realize they are being used as tools to further a larger agenda.

Some people are legitimately confused in their gender, but there's a lot of influencing and misleading of young people, with hatred aimed at the parents trying to prevent what they consider manipulation from occurring. I have tremendous sympathy for the kids who are in need of understanding and counseling over this issue, but not for the school administrators and the governance that allow indoctrination to occur.

Separatism and the need to be right, thinking you know better is part of what prevents us from advancing individually and keeps us in a place of subservience. What gives anyone the right to control another?

Jumping Dimensions Tool 7: Allow Free Will

Free will is a sovereign right. Every one of us has free will. Allowing others their free will to choose and not imposing your will upon them is essential to your growth as well as theirs. You can speak your piece. You can offer a convincing argument. But if they are adults it's up to them to choose how to behave and how to move forward or not to move forward.

You want to take on their karma? I don't think so. You want to make them do something that's against their intrinsic integrity? That's bad on you. Moving into 5D, you leave all the controlling, ungrateful, divisionary people as well as these aspects of your own self behind.

The truly attainable goal is freedom—true, sovereign freedom for yourself and others.

Freedom means you are in control of your own life. Yes there's stuff going on around, threatening to take this or that away. Be secure and stand tight. Do not let enslaved thinking encroach. You have to guard your 5Dness with everything you've got, because people will try to take it from you.

Jumping Dimensions Tool 8: Avoid Energy Vampires

We all have these people in our lives. They sometimes don't realize they're doing it. They're relentlessly needy in their search for validation and a place to dump their negativity. These types of people have to learn to stand on their own and will want to use you as their crutch.

That's 3Dness in the extreme, where you are just as much at fault as they are for not setting them straight or barring them entry to your premises. Can you be a friend from afar? Absolutely, yes. Guard your energy. If you become effected by them, if your mood changes or you begin to view everything through a pessimistic lens, for example then you need distance and boundaries.

Jumping Dimensions Tool 9: Bypass Addictions

Addictions keep you down. Liquor, drugs, excessive food, carbohydrates, sugar, even plastic surgery have been placed before us to clog our processes and keep us from experiencing the true depth of who and what we are.

Addictions keep us in an unsatiated state of always needing more, a space detached from your authenticity. I'm not saying to not enjoy a glass of wine here and there. I sure do. I'm often too much in my head and I prefer the looseness a little bit of wine provides in social settings. But it's not an addiction. If you're using something as a numbing agent or if you can't easily give it up it has to go.

Originally plant drugs were here to take us to an altered state of reality so that we could connect with the different dimensions. India's Vedic philosophers wrote the sacred Rig Veda texts several thousand years ago under the influence of marijuana and ayahuasca. But the drugs since then have been badly altered and must be used with extreme caution, if at all.

For a time drugs were used in a transformative, creative way. Some attest to their benefits in opening the third eye and seeing into other worlds and dimensions. You can't trust that ayahuasca however, won't open doors you will later regret having opened. I know people have done it successfully, but I also know those who regret opening holes in their aura and allowing entry to low dimensional entities.

It's like playing Ouija board, where you're throwing your doors open and saying, come on in! Why chance sabotaging the excellent work you are doing, and going to do, on yourself? You will get to a point where you can experience universes without mind altering substances, with no risk of negative attack.

There is something else an increasing number of young people are doing, perhaps unwitting of its true significance. This is adopting Satanism, witchcraft and occult practices. These lead down very dark roads from which you may never return. Many believe that witchcraft can be good. Keep in mind that nothing that impinges on another's free will is good. People who think it's cool to invite in demons often never come back from the experience. They're gone forever and what is left is a shell.

Phase II: The Physical World

"We are supposed to become a race of leaders—not a race of sheep. We are supposed to be chiefs. That is what they teach their people, nobody falls behind. We all evolve together."
Alex Collier, Andromedan Contactee

Chapter 9: Getting Off The Mountaintop

We've talked about ways to change your thinking and ways of being to lead you towards becoming your best, true, manifesting self. Development of our inner world is essential. In healing ourselves we also heal others. But is this enough? Ignorance of the world we physically inhabit, a world which wreaks harm on innocents, is a form of spiritual sabotage.

It is a sad truth that the world around us is not what we perceive, and beneath a veil of deception lies a hidden cabal of beings who do not value the beautiful essence of love, creativity and extraordinary personal power humans, when left to their own devices, can embody.

Our ascension cannot occur if we remain in darkness. More so, we cannot make the changes to make this world a better place, the place it was meant to be and is capable of being, if we lack the knowledge of what really is going on.

As you move closer to a sense of Oneness you will come to understand how inaction equates to complicity. Inaction not only means knowing something is wrong and not standing up against it, but deliberately ignoring the truth of what is occurring.

As I mentioned earlier, we are engaged in a full on spiritual battle where the very fate of humanity hangs in the balance. Winning this battle cannot occur while living in a state of ignorance or avoidance. Real ascension cannot occur this way either. In other words, no mountaintop sitting allowed.

Does this mean you have to stage demonstrations and picket school boards? Sometimes, yes. Are you supposed to be demonstrating against child trafficking? Maybe, yes. But the cognizance of things and raising the of awareness of those around you is a step towards facilitating change. You cannot consider yourself "ascending" while leaving parts of your self to suffer. For those who suffer are aspects of all of us.

Let me rephrase that. As we ascend and move toward a place of unity consciousness, we begin to comprehend that what happens to another happens to us as well. Planetary ascension cannot occur when parts of the whole are left in abusive conditions. I'm referring to true ascension with the planet being lifted out of slavery consciousness and into a pure and natural state of being. As you move further in your understanding you come to realize that both yours and planetary ascendency are one and the same.

Just as cancer cannot survive in an acidic environment, a person can also not be authentic in an ignorant state.

The Unfortunate Truth

The unfortunate truth is that there exists in the shadows a dark force that has been working against humanity for a very long time. This shadow presence has infected governments, food, health care, religions, banking and education systems. It has kept our minds, bodies and spirits in ignorant and complacent states, out of touch with our selves, our abilities, and our true connections. Left to our own devices we are capable of anything. Under control of this shadow reality, we become slaves.

A full explanation of the players and their tactics would require its own book. In the most concise way possible I will run down the major points here. A public rollout out of information in the form of disclosure is said to be soon coming and may have already hit the light of day by the time this book reaches you. As the structures peel away use the emerging truths to empower you. Now that you know, you will overcome it all.

You have known all along that something was wrong, haven't you? Ignoring it doesn't make it go away.

A Word of Warning

Some of this information may seem extreme and hard to believe, or in the nature of conspiracy theory. For me personally, this has come as a result of 20-odd years of hard research. Everything I relay is verifiable once you conduct your own, accurate, investigations.

The Shadow World Players

The Khazarian Mafia is the world's oldest and most organized secret crime syndicate. They a responsible for, among other things, the system of Babylon money magic which chains us in debt slavery. Despite the fact that many who practice Catholicism will be offended, the Vatican is on the top of the list of those who perpetrate evil. Read the Jesuit Oath if you do not believe me.

Do not look for those who form the shadow world in history books, because according to textbooks, they don't exist. According to mainstream media and politicians they don't exist. That's why you need to look more deeply into these things.

The evil these and other factions have perpetrated on humanity is beyond the imagination of most moral humans. They can only operate in secrecy. The sooner their cover is blown, the sooner the dark aspects of the system will be taken down. The Khazarian Mafia are not Jews, although they will masquerade as such. Like the others, they are an occult group that practices Baal worship, Luciferian black magic, and Satanism.

Multiple Rings

Controlled by unseen hands with front men like George Soros, Henry Kissinger, and Bill Gates to do the dirty work, the system of control has been in operation for hundreds, if not thousands of years. The rings of operations encompass all major governments and 3 letter agencies including the WEF, WHO, UN, FDA, CDC, CPS, IRS, NSA, TSA and more. The illegal Federal Reserve, FEMA, Homeland Security, TSA, and CIA are behind the false flag operations that wreak tragedy on the world populaces and have nearly eradicated our ability to live in harmonious peace. These are mere front agencies for the dark side to accomplish its aims, which is ultimately the enslavement of humanity and the eradication of our free will and freedom.

Their acts of terror are so large that one cannot go into them without sounding like an immense conspiracy theorist. Instead, I will try to present insight into select situations in digestible pieces.

Dark Operations

Those under the influence of these players practice regular dark rituals which involve infant and child torture and sacrifice. For more information on this please see the docuseries I created with LifeSource entitled *Alice in Pedoland*. The link may be found in the back pages.

This unfortunate state of affairs extends to a worldwide pedophilia blackmail operation that holds all people of power in their grip. In this way those holding major positions in government, media, tech, and big pharma around the globe are pulled into the darkness where they are corrupted and controlled.

The Babylon money magic system involves substituting paper certificates for silver and gold and chaining us to a perpetual debt-slavery system that channels us from birth to death into soul-deadening jobs in a never ending debt cycle. The paper they call money has no value. Entrapping us through usurious interest, spiraling debt and financial scams, has enriched families like the Rothschilds and Rockefellers and other members of bloodline families.

The control system extends to the hundreds of thousands who do their bidding out of fear, threats, bribery, ignorance, greed and extortion.

The many murders and wars we have experienced have in

reality been committed in their name and not for the cause of justice and democracy as so many have believed. For now, I call this cabal and their minions, the Dark. I refuse to call them elite. Even globalist is too nice a word. "Parasites" is more fitting.

Bloodlines and "Illuminati"

Illuminati is a term we hear often, yet few really know what it means, thinking that it primarily refers to a dark and mysterious cult comprised of faceless, chanting figures in black hoods. The Illuminati have been around from at least the 17th century, and involves at least 13 bloodline families who have perpetrated a pattern of satanic ritual abuse which feeds on the suffering of others. This is to obtain power, wealth, eternal youth and favor with their god, Lucifer. Even the U. N. has a room dedicated to Luciferian worship as does the Vatican.

We'll talk more later on about their system of programming through Satanic Ritual Abuse (SRA) and how it is used. For now understand that SRA is how they perpetuate evil through the bloodlines. It's why they marry within families. It's why incoming generations of the bloodline families choose to remain in a system that enslaves others. Basically, the Illuminati is a deeply nefarious group that considers humanity their servant. They are part of a network of secret societies working in conjunction with one another and who keep human beings in a state of perpetual enslavement, indebtedness, ill health and ignorance.

Most every American president is from a bloodline family. That does not mean they were practicing nefarious ways themselves, but they were undoubtedly being controlled. It pays to do a little digging on this and some genealogical research.

People who are in power, including all the royals, corporate heads, and politicians come from the bloodline families. Even those who seemingly marry into these families, like Megan Markle and Kate Middleton, are from bloodline families. This extends to Hollywood players. You'll find that the largest celebrities, television producers, agents and directors are all bloodline.

This is because the people within the bloodline families, the ones in power, the ones who control the money and the systems of enslavement, choose to keep it within the family.

Freemasonry, Good or Bad?

There is a lot of misinformation as to whether Freemasons are good or bad. Many people maintain that they do a tremendous amount of good in their communities. So how could they be bad?

In quick summation, Freemasonry on the beginning levels, is indeed good. They do good works. They are shrouded in an aura of Christian morality that many resonate with. In and of that, it's positive.

However, there is another another layer to Freemasonry. As you go into the deeper recesses toward the first 33 degree level and above, the pledges grow increasingly dark in nature. By the time members see the truth they are are sworn in, and stuck because they have pledged not just their own lives but the lives of their families should they leave or speak out about what is going on. There is another level of 33 beyond the first 33 that few know about, that is shrouded in the occult.

By the time the levels below 33 find they have pledged to Lucifer it is too late. There's not a lot of information out there because to be a member and to reveal it will end in death to you and your loved ones. There have been a few noteworthy leaks of information despite this.

Truth is empowerment. Use it for good, and you will be empowered. If you're doing good deeds as a Freemason and you're in the network, just stop. Don't go any further. Don't go to any higher levels. Stay as you are and continue to feed those children, clothe the poor, and do all that good stuff that you're doing.

The Deep State

Deep State is a term you've no doubt heard, possibly in conjunction with coups against governments. The Deep State is a real entity. It's also called the Shadow Government, the Cabal, the Elite, the Globalists, etc.

There's a lot of names involved. The Committee of 300. Illuminati, Freemasons... the Jesuit faction, the Vatican, the Khazarian Mafia...they're all connected. The Deep State organism operates within the offices of our elected officials on every level from the very highest level to the very lowest. People are either considered puppet masters or puppets.

They're either doing the controlling or are being controlled through coercion, blackmail, bribery, threats or plain ignorance. For many people are compartmentalized and really don't have any idea what's going on at the very top.

How do you recognize the world players? If the individual is a member of the Council of Foreign Relations, the Trilateral Commission, the SES, or attend Bilderberg meetings, you can be assured they are part of the Deep State. If heads of state are following the given narrative, such as "Palestine is Bad," "You Must Wear Masks," "Climate Change is Real," "The Covid Vax Prevents Transmission," and so on, they are part of, or being controlled by the Deep State.

It's important to recognize the techniques and sleights of hand as these players operate behind a shield of optics. In other words, they appear to be one thing while they are really something else behind that shield.

Puncturing the Cabal Veil

Among the many cabal tactics, rhetoric stands out as a common technique. Parts of this list come off of the 8chan boards posted by Anonymous. They're all Anons there, for their work is dangerous.

Generalizations

This is making a broad statement that uniformly applies to everything without taking the time to argue. It is the quickest method of creating indoctrinated thinking, such as saying all democrats are libtards or that all Trump supporters are toothless crackheads. Stupid, yes. But generalizations can be very insidious, and used to separate us over issues like racism, feminism, and gender choice.

Gaslighting
From the Alfred Hitchcock movie, *Gaslight*. Taking a page from the narcissist playbook, this is a manipulation used in personal relationships, but also by the Deep State as a control tactic. Gaslighting makes you feel like your thoughts are wrong, unwarranted or insignificant. It's turning things around and blaming somebody for something they haven't done, in the process turning the people they know against them.

Let's say you tell your partner you're really upset about the fact he hasn't supported you and he in turn says, *you're being dramatic. You're so Italian. You're overreacting.* Then he has a sit-down with your parents voicing his concern about your mental health.

That's gaslighting in its common, if not extreme, form. *How about: you're such a conspiracy theorist. Is everything negative with you? Are you ever happy about anything?* That's another form of gaslighting. Gaslighting leaves the victim in a place of having to defend himself against an untruth, an almost impossible thing to do. How do you defend yourself against something that isn't there? Even as you try, the thought has already been planted.

The cabal uses the technique frequently by labelling people as such and such or accusing them of things like acquiring kiddie porn. Once the idea is planted in the minds of the public it never goes away.

Projection
Projection is when a person guilty of something applies it to you, or his opponent, instead of himself. Psychologically speaking, projections are the attribution of one's own attitudes onto others. The thought in psychoanalytical theory is that it is an unconscious defense against anxiety or guilt over knowing you're wrong. When the person you're talking to says that you are generalizing or that your facts are unsubstantiated, realize they are probably projecting their own guilt or lack of knowledge upon you.

Projection is used continuously in politics, so much so that all you have to do is look at the accusers to realize that they are actually referring to themselves.

Misdirection

This technique is smoothly used by politicians these days. That's when they change the conversation to another less important or incendiary topic, so instead of a congressman admitting that he has called for the wall himself on numerous occasions, he would instead say that his political opponents are idiots for calling for the wall. When reminded of the flood of immigrants pouring through porous borders, he will again misdirect and say that he wasn't the one who tore the wall down. Instead of a sitting president admitting his son's laptop contains images of his son with naked, compromised children while shooting up with heroine, he instead reminds everyone how his other son died in Iraq, which he in fact did not do.

False Equivalences

These are logical fallacies. Your cat is orange, so all cats are orange, right? Or, someone is a misogynist because in the 1980s he engaged in locker room talk with somebody who was illegally recording him. He said a bad word that many men have used behind closed doors.

All presidents have had affairs. Every last one of them. Some have had nighttime shipments of little girls and boys. To be calling one out for a much smaller offense is called Hypocrisy 101.

False Flags

This is probably another term that you've heard and are possibly wondering whether it is theory or fact. I assure you, it is not theory.

False flags are operations set up by Deep State entities in order to bring about a change they want to see. 9-11 might be described as one of the biggest false flags we've had, in which the Deep State immediately introduced controls that got us thinking we were being protected. By causing us to fear the bogeyman, in this case Al-Qaeda, we readily gave up our freedoms. They created such fear that we accepted deep controlling limits on our sovereignty.

Fear is one of the biggest methods of control there's ever been. This is why I spend such a large amount of time talking about eradicating it.

False flags have readily occurred and are set up by the Deep State with film crews, advanced tech and crisis actors. It's become such an overused tactic that most of these set ups are now readily spotted by social media warriors. Milton William Cooper was an ex CIA agent who announced the school shooting false flags before they started to occur. These were set to roll out in various schools across the country in order to eliminate the 2nd amendment, which is the right to bear arms. Soon afterwards came Columbine then successive school shootings.

Every time you see somebody shooting students up in a school or people in a crowded location such as a sports marathon or dance club, chances are it's a false flag. There are clues that you can follow. If it involves a disenfranchised young loner whose family disappears right after, chances are it has been set up. Chances are the shooter was hearing voices and was on some sort of psychotropic drugs, info which is wiped from the internet before the incident even occurs.

The Boston bombing was a huge false flag operation. Crisis actors were employed. Ads were circulated about hiring false flag crisis actors before the event. This is not to say there weren't victims. Undoubtedly, people got killed. Some people in Sandy Hook got killed. I'm not saying that children weren't hurt. I am saying that this was deliberately created and set up by the Deep State in order to create an anticipated reaction.

Bill Cooper called them out on this, and said it was coming because this was how they were going to get gun control past the masses who believe in the Constitution and the right to bear arms. Sometime after his revelations Cooper was gunned down in his front yard.

As to false flags and how to identify them: there's almost always a practice operation a day or two before the operation. There are other indicators as well, but know that a false flag is a major event involving the death of innocents while delivering fear and trauma to the public in order to create an anticipated or desired reaction.

Virtue Signaling

There's a lot of virtue signaling going around. Basically this is saying, *I'm good because I say I'm good. Look at what I just did.* It's a house of lies usually, and it's got a political agenda to it. It's insincere and selfish.

Hollywood types are adept at virtue signaling. Look at the female starlets who were saying how wonderful they were because they're, you know, proponents of the "Me Too" movement. You knew by listening to them that they were there to publicize themselves. A virtuous person never signals or tell us how good they are because they're doing good deeds.

Truly good people are working in a selfless manner day and night without telling anyone about it. If somebody's saying they're virtuous, you can bet they're full of it.

Identity Politics

Identity politics is where a group of people who identify with a certain label see themselves as disenfranchised and lobby, riot or saturate the news cycles with complaints of their ill treatment. This is not about humanity. This is about individual groups who put their needs over everyone else's. If anyone is disenfranchised and needs looking after, it's the veterans group. Yet we don't see them employing expensive lobbyists. Instead, we see them helping others despite their overwhelming problems. The issue with identity politics is in identifying with a single group, you are too often disregarding the rights of others. Plus you have to take social engineering into account.

Social Engineering

Social engineering is a construct that grew out of Project Paperclip, which was the influx of the Nazis and their way of being after WWII. Many say we are still fighting that war. Look into the Bush family and their Nazi roots. That's just one family. It goes far deeper and involves alleged pillars of society that includes the Dulles, Morgan Chases, Harrimans, and other banking families.

Social engineering controls society to an ever greater degree through indoctrination, separation and imposed narratives. Climate change is one such imposed narrative. It is neither liberal nor conservative nor Democrat nor Republican. Climate change is a means of controlling the population and is a worldwide, globalist, Deep State effort.

The scientists who spoke out about it were silenced. The media is controlled by these Deep Staters, and the narratives that reach you are the ones they want you to hear.

Tavistock Institute in London is heavily involved in the process, and is behind, among other things, the debasing theories of Sigmund Freud and modern day public relations, which is the art of getting the public to believe the false narratives that further their agendas. Edward Bernays, the father of PR, was Sigmund Freud's nephew.

The Tavistock think tank still controls modern day thought. If we're going to talk about an imposed narrative, look at feminism. I'm an absolute advocate of treating everyone equally. I am absolutely an advocate of women's rights. However feminism was engineered to break up the family unit, to send children into day care earlier, and to double the tax base. Suddenly two people in every home were paying income taxes.

Prior to the 1950s, a double tax base didn't exist. Of course, a strong family unit is a great threat to any sort of control system. On top of that, feminism pits women against men. More separation.

I could go on about how the ghettos were deliberately created to keep the lowest income individuals separate from others and how the fathers were removed from these places and put in jail after drugs flooded the communities.

To all outward appearances the Women's Liberation movement appeared to be addressing wrongs. That is the way the cabal operates: using legitimate complaints as the vehicle to roll out insidious programs. This is just one of many movements being used against us.

Of course good has come out of this in that we have become more aware of what it means to be equal. But when you put down one group at the cost of another, it becomes identity politics at its worst.

Chapter 10: Beneath the Veil

Politics are about separating people and not about representing them. They're about dividing allegiances, diverting attention, and focusing us on a parade of unnecessary things they tell us to worry about. Meanwhile, behind the veil our governors are stuffing their pockets and committing terrible deeds. None of them are acting for the people's interest.

If they were acting in our interest there wouldn't be campaign contributions. Paid lobbyists would not be allowed to influence votes. Senators would be forced to settle issues before taking a holiday. Congress would be paid only for the days they show up. No bill could be passed that wasn't easily read and understandable. No addendums would be slipped into enormous bills and passed without scrutiny. There would be no Federal Reserve. Governors on all levels would take a cut in salary rather than see the people they represent suffer. There would be an oversight committee enacting punishment for politicians who lie or commit insider trading. There would be a time limit before a governor of any kind could accept a position on a corporate board. There would be no stock market investing or insider trading. There would be no offshore accounts. In fact, their finances would be heavily monitored.

The Big Lie

We have been made to believe we have to draw sides when in truth we all want the same thing: safety for our families, good health, nutritious food, financial liberation and personal freedom.

The Big Lie is there is no real difference between a democrat and a republican, a conservative and a liberal or even a communist and fascist. The same money controls all sides. The non-humans on TV, talking heads, yapping talk show hosts, and endless dribble in the media are diversions. The system is designed to divert our attention from the true issue at hand, which is the absolute corruption of global government from the top down, and to focus on what separates us from one another instead. If we were to unite we would be too powerful to overcome.

Every honest politician is turned bad by the system for there is no other way to survive. If you speak out you are eliminated. A sexual indiscretion usually serves well enough. If not, a larger scandal is created, or straight out murder, and the transgressor is taken down.

As long as we have people representing us with compromised interests, they are not our representatives. As long as there is corporate funding of any kind, they are not our governors. They are the corporations' governors. When I use the term governors, I mean all politicians, officials and monarchs, elected, appointed, or ushered in on the strength of their genetics.

When you appoint people to cabinets in return for favors, or when you are bought by powerful lobbyists, you are no longer acting for the people. You are beholden to another interest.

The Media

It's important understand who and what controls the things you see every day, if you are indeed still watching TV or going to the movies or listening to the radio.

As of 2018, it came down to six corporations owning virtually 100% of the media, if not all of it. I'm saying "virtually" for the sake of being fair. The five primary conglomerates are Time Warner, Disney, the Murdoch News Corporation, Bertelsmann of Germany, and Viacom, which was formerly CBS.

Their control spans social media, newspapers, books, TV, Film, radio, and all global web content. It should be noted that all five of these major corporations are corporate members of the Council on Foreign Relations, or the CFR.

The CFR is a think tank that is part of the social engineering programs we've been subjected to, as well as destabilization efforts and takeover of governments. The media conglomerate's fellow members of the Council on Foreign Relations include the CEOs of virtually every large corporation in the Western and Eastern Hemispheres, and present and former government officials.

Somebody whose name you might remember is Zbigniew Brzezinski, whose doctrine calling for U. S. control of the Eurasian landmass, which includes Russia and China, is one of the guiding elements of U. S. foreign policy. It should also be noted that the conglomerates themselves are behemoths. They contribute to both of America's parties, Republican and Democrat, while supporting policies of control and division.

The Reagan, Clinton, Bush administrations, and so on, have enacted progressively greater media deregulation. Obama legalized propaganda. These regulations, once lessened, permitted greater media monopolies, allowing for the very first time, all the media in a single city to be owned by one corporation.

Do you think by listening to Fox versus CBS, you are not being indoctrinated? They're merely two sides of the same coin. Pages would be needed to list the thousands of information outlets controlled by five conglomerates. A few examples will suffice. News Corp owns Fox News, The Wall Street Journal, Barron's Weekly, The London Times, The Far Eastern Economic Review, The New York Post, and hundreds of other large and small city and community newspapers, magazines, and internet outlets. Time Warner owns Time Magazine, Fortune Magazine, People Magazine, Sports Illustrated, CNN News Group, Turner

Network, Warner Brothers Films, DC Comics, Times Online Systems, and much more.

Disney is not just about Mickey Mouse. If you study the international pedophilia blackmail system you'll know that Disney is far more than it seems. Disney owns ABC Television, magazine publishing businesses, Disney Films, Lucasfilms, and a huge number of other media and entertainment enterprises.

How can anyone think they are getting free and honest information?

What's the Answer?

One answer is, use your buying power.

Every once in a while, there does seems to be somebody who is telling the truth. In 2012, the lone voice appeared to be Ron Paul. Those people are generally kept under wraps. In his case he was taken out of the race. If you could follow his true support in the polls, you'd have seen it was far greater than what was reported. The truth is, we need a new way of government. We need governors who are acting for the people. We need to eradicate this current system. The Federal Reserve is not a federal agency but a private one, acting for private interest. It was created as a money-making machine, and the bill to install it was passed in under the publics' noses on Christmas Eve in 1913. Don't believe me. Do your homework.

Lincoln was assassinated for fighting them not for freeing the slaves. Follow the presidents along. Do a search for individual presidents and the Federal Reserve and you'll see they sided with or against them. When they fought them, they were gotten rid of. When they sided with them, they were kept in office.

So what do we do? Vote with your wallets. Become sustainable and stop relying so much on consumer products. Be very selective in the brands you support. Don't feed the machine.

The Federal Reserve

The individuals who succeeded in getting the Federal Reserve implanted took control of our money system. These are the same people who control the IMF, or the International Monetary

Fund, which has succeeded in bringing down country after country by extending credit and then squeezing off that credit. It's a popular tactic.

They did it in Yugoslavia. They did in every country you can think of. Greece, Portugal, Spain and Italy suffered. The fact is nothing is as it seems, including self-imploding countries like Egypt, Syria, and Libya whose rebellions were engineered for profit.

There was once a very edifying document online called the Illuminati Timeline, that follows, step by step, how the West took down regimes, built them back up, pretended to take them down again, and so on. It's a ploy. We're not creating freedom and democracy if we're warring on other countries. We're killing them for personal gain. We are creating impoverishment and destroying infrastructures so we can so that we can go back in and make profit for rebuilding them, as well as put our own colonialism in place. Do you think that we were really looking for weapons of mass destruction in those Iraqi enclaves? No, we were taking down a society.

I say, "we," because our governors are doing it in our name. We have been creating war, hatred, and grief with a purpose in mind. Those who look the other way are complicit.

Not Humans

The people who are orchestrating these things may look like human beings, but they're missing the human component called compassion. Many theories abound about who these individuals are who are running our world and creating war and destruction, but let's just say that, despite their many concerned-looking photo ops, they are lacking the qualities that make us human. They care only about power, money and eternal life.

As I've mentioned, except for one every single person we've had as a ruler in the United States of America as well as the European monarchies is connected by birth if you trace the bloodline back. You as a citizen of this world need to take responsibility for understanding these things. The fact is a small group of individuals control this planet and have for a very long time.

Now, whether you believe that these are ET's or reptilians or just powermongers gone amuck is up to you. The various theories out there each have their own level of believability. One thing that is irrefutable is that they use the system to control us through fear. Fear that we're not going to have enough to pay our bills, to restore our health. Fear that we'll lose our property or our children. Fear of war. Fear of weather patterns. Fear of nuclear holocaust. Fear of industrial disasters. Fear of food shortages. The list goes on.

Fake Money

Who said money needs to create interest? Who said you need to borrow money for interest?

Lincoln didn't, and he wanted to formalize the fiat money system, where money was lent to whoever needed it and was paid back without interest. What a revolutionary idea. No interest. Interest which goes, by the way, to the bankers controlling the Federal Reserve not to American coffers.

As we keep borrowing, our money is being siphoned off to the bankers, the JP Morgans, the Chases, the Rockefellers and the Rothschilds. It's a very checkable fact. All the information contained herein is verifiable. While you still have an internet at your disposal as well as books and libraries, you should check into all I am telling you. The truth is out there to find.

Try this. When it comes to money, you must eradicate fear of not having enough in your life. I know you have rent or a mortgage to pay. You have to buy food. You have to get clothing for your children. The answer is to try to go back to basics as much as you possibly can. A lot of us living in urban areas will find this especially hard, but if we go back to collective growing resources, to the way our grandparents lived in communities and helped each other, that's the answer.

Maybe it won't happen in our lifetimes, but we can start. I'm not saying to eradicate luxury, I'm not saying not to travel or to enjoy the finer things in life, but to discern what's truly valuable and to opt for that in your life instead of the things others tell us are valuable.

This means to stop the high grade consumption. Do you really need that new dishwasher? Do you need that super duper high speed cappuccino machine? Do you need the excess we're used to living with? If you travel to other countries beyond the resort areas, you'll find others subsist well on far less than we have. They travel more, see friends more, enjoy family more, and work fewer hours. They also spend far less money buying plastic items from China.

The 1%

In many places in the world you'll see a level of excess is missing, except for those who have become Westernized. Consider this. Less than 1 percent of the earth's population control 99.999 percent of the world's wealth. What's wrong with this picture? Why are people starving? Why are billionaire stars asking for handouts for disaster victims instead of digging into their own pockets?

Consider the fact that the wealthy people asking for money to help raise awareness or send food or aid a myriad of other philanthropic efforts, could meet the world's needs quite easily with a tiny portion of the wealth that is controlled by the one percent. Our rulers, our governors, and our icons are hypocrites, pawns, and villains, and the multiple disasters you have seen where people were asked to send money have been yet another means of wealth transfer. This is where money and property is transferred from the poor to the increasingly wealthy. COVID was another time this occurred. The real estate disaster of 2008 was another.

Many events throughout history, which looked like a natural occurrence, were actually wealth transfers.

These people who are asking for money or who are telling us that we have to be vaccinated, for instance Bill Gates, who comes from a line of eugenicists, are doing so for financial reward. Why do people listen to Bill Gates about vaccines? Vaccines do not prevent illness. A strong immune system prevents illness. There is a second set of vaccines available to the rich that do not contain toxins. The politicians all got out of the COVID vax mandates. They have their own biodynamic farms and underground shelters for when the expected turmoil over what they have done to us breaks out.

Personal Wellbeing

The only way to confer immunity is through getting sick and fighting it. Mother's milk boosts immunity.

When you don't breastfeed your baby, you're consigning them to weakness right from the start. I'm not putting down mothers who legitimately cannot breastfeed, and there are ways of combating this by using colostrum from goat milk, for instance, which is the closest to human in its composition.

Never listen to authorities who say it's okay to not breastfeed. In fact, never listen to authorities if you can help it, especially when they say something that doesn't sit right with you.

We have destroyed our personal health through parasitic infestations, toxins that create disease, processed foods, lack of sunshine, pharmaceuticals, and emotional stress. What's the biggest cause of emotional stress? Fear. As we have discussed, fear is built into the fabric of our society. Fear that our unborn child won't get into the right nursery school unless they register on time. Fear that our children in grammar school will not get into the proper junior high school if we take them out of school for a vacation. Yet a family vacation might enlighten them far more than any school program could.

Fear that if we do not pass the standardized tests everyone is so terrified of, the school will lose its funding. Fear that if children do not pass those tests they are not going to go to a proper college. Of course, if they do not get into the proper college we know for a fact they're not going have a proper job opportunity when they get out. Do you see how fear drives most everything we do?

The truth is, the job that you get out of college is going to put you right back on that track of fear. Do you really want to go inside the corporate structure? If so, why? To make money? What's your true joy in life? That's what you need to follow, not the most lucrative path. If you find your true joy in life, you're going to make the most with what you give back to the world. You also won't die saying, "What did I do it all for?" You won't change who you intrinsically in your path to get there. Because that's the reality of it.

I personally saw tons of idealistic NYU grads leave the school, stars in their eyes, saying, "I am going to change the world. I am going to help the world." They became Wall Street brokers and bankers and execs just like everyone else. Then they got ground down inside the machinery and changed inside just like everyone else.

The most happy people in the world are those who are doing what they want, what they were put on this planet to do. Sometimes this doesn't include making a lot of money. We know money is valuable. We all want it. I am not going to tell you not to get some. But, what would you do with the money? Buy boats and other vehicles, bigger houses, better possessions? Money is important to keep families together and to pay rent and food bills. Clothes are important, as are electronics, and vehicles for transportation. Add in a heat source, gas, entertainment and vacations. A reasonable level of luxury would be lovely. Beyond that what would you do with that money? Would you take it and empower the world around you? Like Jesus said, "Give a man a fish and feed him for a day. Give him a fishing pole and feed him for a lifetime." Well, Jesus didn't say that exactly, but it was something like that. I think it had to do with seeds, but you get the picture. If you're going to change the world, how are you going to do that? And, where is your money and effort best spent?

Chapter 11: Your Physical Self

In addition to being very spiritual, my family was holistic. We ate natural foods and practiced natural forms of healing. Sometimes things like surgery were necessary but the general course of action was to heal everything we could without a doctor visit. Nowhere was our difference from others more apparent than in the school lunchroom.

When I was in elementary school, let's just say that the go-to lunch box items were baloney on white bread and sometimes, if you were lucky, PB&J. Now I know for a lot of you, that is really digging into the past and may seem irrelevant.

If you look around lunchrooms these days, you will see mostly packaged foods like Lunchables, which are filled with chemicals and are as far from the natural source as can be. The foods that kids eat in lunchrooms across the country hardly resemble food anymore, and that that includes cafeteria service.

My family mostly ate green things, which served as a point of ridicule for my classmates. Through the pain of ostracism I came to understand that being different wasn't such a terrible thing. This is where I began to learn to be strong in who I was.

I grew up hearing about the teachings of Adele Davis, who was one of the forerunners of the organic movement, while my own grandfather homesteaded in New York before there were communities out there, tending a thriving organic farm that he used to feed his family, the neighbors, nuns from the local convent, and anyone else who came by.

He didn't make money from any of this. The man lived by his wits and knowledge. He was an inventor of sorts who rigged up his own solar panels and an endless variety of farming equipment. One of the things that fascinated me as a child was an old tennis racket he used to bat insects off the fruit and vegetables. He would never, ever, use a pesticide. He grew up in Manitoba, Canada, where farming was their way of life. I can only imagine that our ancestors would also have never have dreamt of using a pesticide.

Sustainability

I would spend summers on Grandpa's farm, not every summer, not every day but every once in a while. He would point out vegetables and explain how to grow them. There were some tough financial times experienced by my family. My father was in an industry that was hit hard by the recession several times over, and many times we found ourselves the recipients of Grandpa's help.

We would go over there and pick bags and bags of little tomatoes. My mom would turn these into delicious soups and sauces. The most amazing thing were grandpa's zucchini squashes. The zucchini were no less than 6 or 7 inches in diameter and they were delicious. It's hard to imagine this, but they were a good 20 inches or more in length. Now, you may say that this is impossible. Did you ever see the film, "Sleeper?" I kid you not, Grandpa's vegetables seemed like that. One zucchini mixed with pasta fed us for a week.

I'd like to tell you a little a hint, a little truth that Grandpa shared with me. He said he used to "scavenge" in the neighborhood. At one time there were horses and cows in the streets, or at least there were in his youth, and that's where he got the droppings that he used to fertilize the garden. Sometime after that I suppose he moved on to the more conventional ways of buying cow manure in a bag, or maybe he used droppings from local animals. No one really knows for sure, but his produce was awe inspiring.

Enter Monsanto

Of course, Grandpa generated his own seeds year after year. He perfected his own garlic, his own butternut squash, corn, asparagus, tomatoes and much more. Everything was hand sown, raised, and harvested by him, and it was quite a large farm for a man who maintained it by himself with only an odd helper here and there. So this was a little tiny bit of my upbringing. You can imagine my pain and outrage over how Monsanto and it's paid government lackeys nearly eradicated organic farming across the globe. Mass suicides of farmers in India, strong-arming small and large countries the world over to use Monsanto's GMO, pesticide-ridden, non self-propagating seeds, have resulted in yielding toxic crops which today contain barely any of their true nutritional value.

As for my own health, I had the good fortune to have parents who were enlightened and who knew that adulterated food was harmful to the body.

All my friends, well, let's call them not friends, but classmates who ostracized me over this, had their baloney on white bread or Wonderbread, which was enriched flour that makes you fat. While they had those things I had stone-ground bread, sprouts, dark green leafy lettuce and some kind of meat or God-knows-what that my mother found at the health food store. My parents were pushing the poverty level at that time, so we ate whatever they could get at the health food store, of which there was only one in our area.

My mom used to get quite a bit of her nutritional help from Pearl, who ran that store. I hated going there because I'd end up sitting on the floor for hours where my mom got enlightened on things like whole proteins, because of course there were few books available, other than those by Adele Davis and a couple of other writers. How do you feed a family when you don't have money to spend on natural foods? You need a mom who is a wizard at making something from nothing, which I was blessed to have.

We did go through a vegetarian phase when there were no vegetarian products to be had, and my mom ended up boiling soy beans that she attempted to pass off as turkeys and other items. This did not go very far with us. If you have ever tasted these little pustules they pretty much came down to eating boils, or toe fungus or something else revolting. We were young and because we did not stand for this, we eventually went back to meat. Other than that, I would say my mom is a miracle worker.

Today's families have no such issues. There are tons of healthy options for those who choose to go off meat. What you must avoid are the Bill Gates *Beyond Meat* products and those like them. These are highly toxic to the human body. Please do not take my word for this. Do your research. Go past the gatekeeper of Google and other mainstream sources and look for real information. It is out there, I assure you.

A Health Mission

These things being said, when my own children were born, I was on a mission to keep them as healthy as possible. The reasons for this were manifold. The world was changing. Multiple vaccinations were prevalent. I learned that vaccines were not effective, that the disease die-off charts were altered, that they contained lethal toxins, and were not tested properly. There were also no accurate long range tests that were not in some way manipulated, not to mention that the existing test data was skewed. Suffice to say at that time I felt through deep research and soul searching that the best way to go was to not vaccinate my children. At this juncture I hold that conviction tenfold. Vaccines have grown to be far worse than they were then, and even more dangerous.

Being a young mother, and quite concerned that I was now leaving my children open to the possibility of illness and other dire things doctors like to scare you with, like diphtheria, whooping cough, polio. I undertook a search to find out how to best keep my children healthy. If we were not going to vaccinate them, and this took quite a lot of convincing on my part since my husband was not at all on the same page, how were we to equip them to fight off diseases?

The answer was actually quite simple and it goes back to my grandfather's farm. You want to make sure their immune system is not compromised in any way. This is still the best way to fight off disease to this day. This is the best advice anyone can give you in terms of your own personal health. Now, what are the main stressors? What are the main things that compromise an immune system?

You're not going to like this unless you've already been open to this way of thinking but here is number one: medicines. Medicines of all types create more problems. There is no medicine, and I'm talking all pharmaceuticals, those that are bought over the counter as well as those prescribed by your doctor, that does not have a side effect and never has any pharmaceutical ever cured anything. These are simple truths. Now some of you are saying, "Well, there are reasons to take them and there are some occasions..." I'll leave that open for you to decide. But do know this, that for every issue that you or your children are facing, there is a natural solution. Sometimes it does take a little more work. In the end, I assure you, the outcome will be much better.

Eliminating The Stressors

The fact is, medicine does not cure disease. It never has. It never will, and only creates worse problems that need additional treatment, because the trillion dollar pharmaceutical/health care industry will never cut off their money supply by curing you. You'll see if you don't already, the world runs on money. America is not the pillar of virtue we believe our forefathers bequeathed us, despite so many having given up their lives to that end. As far as medicine, I know many of you are saying that you know this or that person who was cured by chemotherapy, radiation, etc. Chances are that if the patient survived chemotherapy they were young and healthy before the cancer stuck. It is a known fact that cures for cancer exists and have for many years. Look up the numerous people who have beaten the disease by changing their lifestyles to eliminate stress and going all raw. That is one way to begin. Many cures exist. Many cures for every disease exists. Unfortunately, many of these cures are found within the indigenous cultures that are slowly being eliminated from the planet. The knowledge is out there if you look for it hard enough. In every situation you need to be discerning and to use your own best inner guidance. Charlatans abound in all areas and the natural health area is no exception.

For now, we need to know how to protect ourselves from disease, especially our young children whom we decide not to vaccinate, or whom we do vaccinate.

Pharmaceuticals are one of the main stressors that compromise our immune system. The next would be adulterated food and by that I mean processed food, or food that is not in its whole, organic state. "Organic" gets us into another issue because what is labeled organic in the stores is not organic. The FDA in its infinite wisdom and of course at the time the head of the FDA was a former pharmaceutical CEO, pulled a fast one, because Wal-Mart was a heavy lobbyist and still is, and they along with the other chain retailers across the country wanted to put organic food on their shelves. But organic is expensive and their consumer base wouldn't buy expensive products, a fact that had been shown through market research. So, what to do? They lobby the FDA to relax the organic food standards.

This way, they could have something that is slightly organic, slap the label on it, and pass it off as real, allowing the rest of us to feel better about the sugar and glyphosate-laden "organic" cereal they're passing off in Target as being good for our children. It's not the truth. When it comes to organic food what we want is the whole organic product that was in my grandfather's garden. How do we get that, when acquiring it is becoming increasingly difficult, and when the government machinery has all but eradicated our ability to obtain true organic food? If you watched the movie *Food, Inc.* then you've got a pretty good idea of what's going on.

But the problem remains, how do we get organic food into our diet? If you don't grow it yourself, with filtered, purified water, with no fertilizers and no pesticides, where do you get it?

Making a Change

You're going to have to find a local farm and you will have to check into them as to what they truly use in their farming practices. Natural is not organic. Then you get together with your neighbors and form a buying co-op, which sounds difficult but once it's done, is quite easy. You can look into organic food co-ops online. If there isn't one where you live then you can form one or create a neighborhood garden where people have equal shares. If this doesn't work, look into hydroponic vertical gardening. This method allows you to grow the largest amount of food possible in the smallest square footage, in your basement or garage with some grow lights, all year round. An alternative to hydroponics is aquaponics, which adds fish in a self-contained ecosystem. Of course a fishing rod serves very well. This will supply you and your family with a supply of non-adulterated produce and protein. You can stay alive and healthy this way with very little cost. Incidentally, you will need organic heirloom seeds and a source of filtered water. For the former, find a seed distributer that has been in business for many years, has not been bought out and is not one of the companies capitalizing on people's fears. For filtered water, reverse osmosis remains the most trusted method, although there are very many theories on how to produce the best water.

Continuing on the subject of water, it is advisable to get your water tested and to obtain the particular filters you may need to eliminate or reduce the harmful substances it may contain. If you live on or near shale formations, which includes about 75% of the United States, make sure to test for hazardous fracking chemicals such as benzene, lead, mercury and strontium, to name a few. If you live in a city you have it easier because regular water analysis tests are mandatory, and posted online. For those of you still in the dark about fluoride, it is not at all necessary to keep your teeth cavity free. Quite the contrary, it is a fraud perpetrated on the public to keep us stupefied, controllable and disconnected from our spiritual selves. You may be familiar with fluoride's deleterious effect on our pineal glands, which are in essence, our third eyes. Studies have shown that remote villages that have never had their water fluoridated have the best teeth. Fluoride is a toxic waste product known to cause, among other things: dementia, severe retardation, lowered IQ, cancerous tumors, muscle disorders, ADD, ADHD, and on and on. Get a filter that is proven effective in reducing fluoride by at least 99%. Nothing less will do.

To put a finer point on processed foods, we've got to be diligent about allergen and toxins such as refined sugars, wheat, and dairy. The body can grow weak fighting these things off day after day, leaving it too taxed to fight disease.

With regard to sugars, unprocessed raw honey that is never heated is a good way to go. Not heating carries over to your tea or coffee. Honey produces toxins when heated. Organic stevia is another well received product. I cooked with it for years and my kids never knew I wasn't using sugar. I did not necessarily like it as an adult and have since found out is used in tropical climates as a means of birth control. I really didn't like the aftertaste, so I have experimented with other sugars such as erythritol and xylitol. Erythritol, however creates quite a bit of stomach distress and is not the natural substance it's touted to be. Xylitol, although I use it, still warrants investigation as to potential side effects.

Monk fruit is used by many people, but still carries a bit of an aftertaste in my opinion. That does not mean you won't like it. So, what does that leave us with? True maple syrup from trees that have not been treated with pesticides would be an excellent way to go along with the raw honey.

When talking about stevia, notice I did not say "Truvia," which is a synthetic product being passed of as Stevia. It should go without saying that your children should never have artificial sweeteners or sodas of any kind. Sodas contain phosphates among other poisons, and leach calcium from bones. Agave, which grew popular fast, is laden with high fructose corn syrup, although the labels do not say so. You need to check the manufacturers on this. High fructose corn syrup is an extremely toxic allergen that should not be consumed by anyone, least of all children.

Lethal Substances

Back to the stressors that compromise our immune system, we've got vaccines, a topic which deserves its own book, but for now, it is vital to understand that these harmful substances do not create immunity but instead create lifelong problems, illness, and death. This is an enormous topic and research has been done by a great many people. Contrary to popular belief, it is within our legal right in the States to refuse to vaccinate our children. At the time of this writing 45 states allow a religious exemption. This involves signing a simple form that vaccinating your child goes against your religious beliefs, and filing this form with your school administrator. This same form can follow them to college.

What's next? Environmental toxins, with which we are now being besieged. We have mercury, cadmium, lead, barium, fluoride, strontium and a full array of other lethal toxins coming in from practices like fluoridated water, fracking, and chemtrails, which involve toxins being deliberately sprayed into our environment. You might think that chemtrails, and some of these other things, are in the order of conspiracy theory. To the contrary, they are intentional, and they are real. Chemtrails are extremely common and most of us don't even recognize that the white plumes being sprayed over our heads every single day is intentional. Almost all cases of Epstein Barr, Morgellons, even Lyme (Borellia) and also AIDS are being spread by the use of toxins and nano-technology in the air, in our water, and in our food. Lyme is not transferred solely by ticks, and AIDS is not transferred solely by intimate contact. There is a growing list of chronic illnesses being caused by these deliberately disseminated toxins and many of these are contained in the chemtrails that are raining down on us in increasing amounts. Chemtrails are NOT contrails, which are harmless steams of vapor released by jets.

Going forward, emotional stress is another of the immune

killers. Now, we're all going to experience stress and there's meditation and yoga to alleviate it.

What is easy to master, and what is being forced on us in an unnatural manner, is fear-based stress. As I have mentioned all too frequently, fear is not a natural condition. It is being manipulated by the forces controlling us.

I do not pretend to have all the answers regarding these things, but there is a reason I have put so much emphasis on eradicating fear. Fear is deliberately cultivated. If not eradicated fear will kill you. The opposite of fear is love. Send every difficult situation that arises in your life, love. Love makes fear go away. Unconditional love is the answer to everything.

Chapter 12: Health Freedom

Another travesty has been perpetrated across the nation, that of the drugging of our children. Almost all American children are on pharmaceuticals, and the rest of the world is following suit. There are many schools of thought as to why, but I'm going to give you an overview derived from my personal observations and experience.

The Schools

What is wrong with our school systems? The way children are taught is antithetical to how they actually learn. Not all of our children fit into the learning pattern, and they present a problem in the public school system or the private schools who conform to standardized tests. The students must perform on these tests, or the school will not receive funding. Teachers have little or no leeway with how and what they teach, and parents and kids have less.

If the child doesn't fit into the box, if they are independent thinkers, if they are unruly—they will be made to fit in. Why are they unruly? Are they bad kids or are they acting out because they've been given all sorts of toxins in their foods and environments, including the poisons in vaccines? Sugar is a huge offender, as are allergies to things like dairy and wheat. Dairy is a toxin. Get it out of your child's diet in all forms. Get out sugar, which includes fruit juice. They may not eat for a few days while you are changing their diet, but they will eat eventually.

Drugging our Children

Back to Ritalin and Aderall and the ADHD /ADD scam. A scam that now includes psychotropic drugs for schoolchildren, as the medical community is widely adding these and other dangerous hallucinogens to their lists of "treatments." If a child thinks and behaves in a way that is different, and expresses opinions that do not conform to the curriculum, he is ruled a troublemaker in need of drugs. A lot of these children at a very early age sense they are being quashed and fight back in their own way, which is often by being disruptive. These children are also made to sit still for hours without adequate outdoor time or physical activity.

There are other of reasons for disruptive behavior. There could be upsetting things going on in the home. There could be upsetting things happening in the school room. Every parent needs to be aware that there are thinkers and spiritual souls among us, who at very early ages are being deprived an outlet. This applies to all children, but there are some who resist more than others.

These children are put on drugs, and before you know it, they are compromised, conformist, and thinking inside the box, thrown into the rat race with everyone else.

What do you do about it? First thing is you change the child's diet, fast, and completely. If he is vaccinated, then homeopathy is one way to counter ill effects, and you'll have to consult a classical homeopath for that. When using homeopathy, stick to classical only, for when you start mixing the remedies they become ineffective and treat the symptom only. It's when they lose effectiveness that the medical community has just cause to say it doesn't work. The fact is, classical homeopathy works. This has been my experience over the years. I've wasted a lot of time and money with homeopaths who have mixed remedies, while classical does not mix.

Healthy Bodies

How do we address ADD and ADHD? Chiropractic is very important in all stages of our lives, but it's particularly helpful to young children in getting their alignments balanced and neural passages cleared. There are many other forms of helpful therapies, including cranial sacral, and acupuncture. Start with the basics. The basics are a whole healthy diet, with no sugar or diary or white flour. Remove all additives. Eat only unprocessed, non-GMO whole foods. This is difficult to do, but not impossible.

If you have to starve your child to get them to start eating healthy foods, know that it is for their own good, and it is the best thing you will do for them in the long run. Try to eliminate wheat, and especially gluten, which as everyone is now realizing, is incredibly toxic to our bodies. Young children are often allergic to it. Dairy is a huge allergen, but soybeans are genetically modified, so you have to be careful about finding a substitute milk. Same with rice milk and almond milk. Organic coconut milk is a great solution. It tastes great and is very healthy. Finding a milk that works for your family calls for experimentation. When my kids were young I rotated milks. Once, my son caught me pouring some alternative milk into a regular milk container. "What are you doing? he asked, ever suspicious of my food methods. When he understood what I was doing, he stopped drinking that milk. So much is psychological with children. You must always be on your toes.

When my kids were very young, I had them on organic goat milk, which was not hard to get. Goat milk is the closest thing to mother's milk in its genetic structure. With eliminating dairy, there are many pitfalls to watch out for and I have stepped into all of them. We have to look for a very organic unmodified whole product to give them.

Next, get them off medicine of all types. Eliminate stressors like fighting in the home. Don't fight in front of the children or within earshot. If there are other things going on, be aware that your child is incredibly emotionally sensitive, far more than you may realize.

Public schools in particular are notorious for making children who don't fit in the box feel stupid. I know what they do and have seen it happen. They make kids feel deficient in an early grade and it never goes away. Co-educate as much as you possibly can. I am not talking tutors so they can do better in the school system, I am saying to offer alternate sources of knowledge so they can be empowered and learn real things. If you can, teach them at home yourself, so that you know that they are getting their ideas heard. Homeschooling is often a wonderful way to go.

Drop Expectations

Back to school and the real problem, which is what to do about them passing the test, so that they can get into the better school, so that they can then get into a better college —these are only areas of concerns if you want your whole life regimented and if you want to do what everyone else does. The truth is, life is very different from what you believe it is when you have young children.

Your kids are going to follow their own path no matter what. There is nothing you can do to change who they are. Let me put that a different way. If you have your hopes set on Harvard, let me tell you, Harvard is not what it's cracked up to be. Harvard may be the very worst place for your child, and the same goes for Princeton and other Ivy League schools. I have a relative who is a counselor at one of these institutions. He says that suicidal tendencies are rampant among those who feel they don't fit in. Always look deeper than how things appear on the surface.

Schools are turning out people who are fitting into the system and perpetuating what isn't working in our society.

You have to choose what's best for you and your children, but the point is to rethink the structure that frames your life. The answer might be different from what you think it is. Take a look at what exists outside your mindset by forcing yourself to consider alternatives.

Whatever you do, you should not bend to pressure from school administrators and teachers as so many have unfortunately done, and put your child on drugs in order to ensure academic success. While their grades may be positively affected, the emotional and physical toll can be irrevocable.

Please do accept and apply all that's been said here when it comes to putting young people on drugs of any kind, psychotropics included. Depression and other so-called mental illnesses can arise from any of the aforementioned items, and can be an indication of deep physical toxicity or a chemical imbalance that can be improved with natural treatment. This toxicity also comes from subliminal programming, particularly smartphones and video games. It's wise to do everything possible to keep your child off drugs. Drugs always have side effects, and more often than not, they worsen the problem.

Health Freedom

We need to talk more about health freedoms before moving on from this section. When we are forced to vaccinate without a recourse, when we are forced to administer drugs to our children, when children are kidnapped by hospitals who force medical treatment upon them, when we are forced to eat inorganic, artificially produced, non-labeled GMO foodstuffs—because to label it would cause people to say, "Whoa, why are you labeling, is there something wrong with it?" we are not a free society. Bill Gates has now issued a product called Apeel, which is not labeled and is going to be on every organic product in your grocery store unless the store or chain opts to ban it.

When we are forced into medical insurance programs, with our every financial and medical statistic recorded, when farmers are not allowed to grow their own organic produce and must use Monsanto's artificially produced seeds, when your organic vegetable garden is declared illegal and forcibly taken down, when your raw milk producer is shut down and criminalized for providing a product that his customers want because pasteurization kills all the good things in your milk —you are not free.

These things and worse are occurring across the globe. Anyone who thinks they are put in place for our own good needs to take a closer look.

The Company Line

Examine the people who are creating these rules and regulations. These are individuals with ties to corporations that are profiting from these endeavors. I can't stress this enough. Don't follow the company line. Look at who is saying what. Look at the truth, and investigate. We are rapidly approaching a non-free society and not just in our health freedoms.

Chapter 13: Living Unprogrammed Lives

Now that you've gotten a sense of what has been going on without your knowledge, what do you do about it? We are not helpless. We are not at the mercy of would-be controllers. Becoming aware is an enormous step and there are actions you can take to pull yourself out of the matrix of deceit.

Living an Unprogrammed Life #1: Remove TV

Yes, you love your favorite TV show. You love this; you love that. You can get virtually every show you have ever dreamed of including your current shows, without ads and commercials, online for free once you figure it out how to do it. Once you find your TV shows, and begin watching them without commercials, you've taken a small step away from indoctrination. You are still being brainwashed through enter "trainment," however. You will soon find that there really aren't that many shows you have to watch. Your list will go down to maybe one or two and then maybe only one that you want to follow. You'll see that weaning yourself off TV is not as hard as you think.

Living an Unprogrammed Life #2: Conscientious Consumerism

Double check every purchase you make. Ask yourself, "Do I really need that?" I am not saying I don't love beautiful clothes. I love beautiful shoes. I mean, I do have too many shoes and I freely admit it. I try to keep my purchases in check and I am trying extremely hard to determine what I do need and what I don't. Consumerism is all around us. Black Friday, Grey Thursday and Cyber Monday are tools to make us think we need more things. It is zombie consumerism and we can say no to it. Buy only what you need and boycott those companies who push negative agendas.

Living an Unprogrammed Life #3: Desexualize Your Kids

The next thing is to understand that we are immersed in a culture of sexualization. Kids are becoming oversexed at younger ages, a sign of the destruction of society. This is not bible-thumping mumbo jumbo. This is about taking a good look at what is happening around us and why. As girls and boys become sexually active at ever younger ages, they also become consumers at increasingly younger ages. The widely publicized debauchery of pop stars and social media influencers, and the over-bombardment of sexual images, has all but eradicated the concept of age-appropriate monogamous sex with a loving partner. The inherent joy and divinity therein has been reduced to ridicule. When we experience the crumbling values of a once moral society, what is left? I know many people feel that if you homeschool your children they're not going to be socialized properly. Perhaps you think you're not equipped, or don't have the time because of your job or career. This is where community comes in, or a supervised tutor while you work from home.

Living an Unprogrammed Life #4: Support Local Government

If we go back to talking about government for a moment, government should be kept at a level closest to you as possible. The more removed the government is from you personally, the more automated and impersonal it becomes, and the less say you have with your governors. There has been a movement for states to become their own governments and not remain beholden to a federal government. At the very least we can make sure that those we elect to local governments have our interests in mind.

Living an Unprogrammed Life #5: Dump the Brainwashing

Everyone is subjected to brainwashing in one form or another. Where do we get it? We get it from the internet. From TV. We get it from film. We get it from the media. We get it from our friends. We get it from politicians. We get it by watching the news. School is possibly the biggest source of brainwashing there is.

As brainwashing comes at you from every possible direction, it is important to get back to your own source, your intuition and your brain. Your best intellectual sense must be combined with intuition and heart. This is the pathway to your personal development and ascendance.

Living an Unprogrammed Life #6: Vibrational Harmony

Discernment is a combination of head and heart. Some might describe this as a combination of intuition and analysis, or intellect with spiritual divination, or leading with the heart, or head, depending on what your particular balance is.

Some like to say it's left brain, right brain thinking. Left brain is the analytical side, right side being more intuitive and creative. I find discernment is a mixture of all of the above. You must find your own particular balance and combination. Personally, I use analysis and deep research as a way of getting into the truth, or at least an understanding of what the truth might be. What does this mean, using analysis? It means digging deeply until you uncover the real truth minus bias or agenda.

This entails drilling down until you get answers that satisfy you. This means they vibrate in an intuitive way. You're looking for vibrational harmony or resonance. Everything you've learned on the way down these multiple rabbit holes is leading you to this place of vibrational harmony.

Chapter 14: Honing Your BS Meter

How do we go about finding this head/heart balance? Is the intellect the starting point? For some, the heart is the starting place. Something just feels right. You just have a sense of knowing. At times I would feel very annoyed by certain people on social media. I just couldn't listen to them. Their voices were too grating, too annoying, or they just felt wrong. They were too egotistical, too ignorant, too slow, too fast. I thought I was just being New Yorky and intolerant. In time, the people that I was intolerant of proved to be disinfo agents. This happened time and time again. Remember, I've been going down these rabbit holes for a very long time. What I learned was that my sense of annoyance was a way of indicating that these people were not vibrating with me. It was my first clue that my BS meter was on high setting.

Their truth, if it was truth, wasn't my truth. This was a very intuitive thing and I had to learn to recognize it, appreciate it, and accept it. Now it's part of my being. My methods have changed and I don't spend as much time on research because the world's changed. But my intuition is strong. Many others have rapidly growing intuition as well, in no small part due to the phenom known as Q.

Love it or hate it, the individuals behind Q brought millions of researchers to the table. Q's information, which began in 2016 and was largely delivered in code, provided clues as to what to search for in compact form. The anonymous posters known as Anons on 8chan, the precursor to 4chan, picked up on the Q "drops" and conducted research that millions followed. However you choose to look at it, Q helped initiate an enormous awakening.

Regardless of the source, we have to use our discernment and not simply trust that what we're being given is correct. You've got to keep drilling down. You've got to find what's resonant with you, but only once you understand the situation.

Question Everything

Some people have a very developed sense of intuition and instantly come up with answers that prove correct. For those who are developing their intuitive sense, this is something that bears repeating: You must keep your mind open to all interpretations and analyses. You're now probably thinking, *how on earth do I do that*? You do this by holding no belief sacred. Unquestioned belief systems cage you in the matrix.

Yes, I believe in certain things. I believe there is a God. I believe there is a Universal Creator. I call this force, which is neither male nor female but possibly both, God or Source. My concept is probably not everyone else's concept of God. I refer to this force as Source and sometimes as the Universe. It's up to you to keep your mind open to all sorts of interpretations and analyses. Unless you do this your BS meter will be stuck on a low setting.

Every single thing we have been taught is not necessarily correct. In fact it most probably is incorrect. The answer is to question everything. I know I've said this before and it's becoming another cliche. I mean it, though. *Question everything.*

No Sacred Cows

In the writing field, editors have a saying, "don't hold any sacred cows." That means that those incredible words you toiled over deep into the night may not be as perfect as you thought. You must be ready to purge them if they don't work. Is this process painful? Yes, if you let it. But slashing and burning what doesn't serve the whole elevates your work. The same goes for your limiting beliefs. Open your mind to different interpretations and analyses. Slash and burn those sacred cows until you come down to empirical truth.

You do this by subjecting every one of your cows to examination. That means you inspect everything you arbitrarily accept as fact.

The fact is, there are no facts. Talk about your mind twisters.

De-Limit Your Beliefs

Limiting beliefs include things like, *My church is the only way to heaven. My government cares about the people.* Or, *We need banks because they have to hold our money.* How about reversing your thinking to: *we don't need money?* There are far better ways of commerce. Here's another belief reversal: religions were created as systems of control. Here's another: The trillions of dollars in debt is not a real thing. Fiat is fake. It is based on nothing. They print money up.

How about the limiting belief that we are anything less than sovereign beings? In other words, that we can't determine our own fates, or our own futures? Yes, we can. We can determine what's right for us and our families. Our rights aren't given to us. They are intrinsic to us. They are inalienable and cannot be violated. They are part of human law, or God's law.

How about the belief in the States that we are a democracy? In fact, America is a constitutional republic. A democracy cedes control to others. A republic keeps the voting power in the hands of the people. At least we were a constitutional republic until being unlawfully reformed as a corporate entity in 1871 by the banking cabal, designating each one of us as commodities.

Here's more. Jesus, or Yeshua, was born on December 25th. Or, killing infidels will send you to heaven. That your appendix is unnecessary. That your uterus is unnecessary once you're finished giving birth. That dementia is part of the life cycle. That sex diminishes with age.

No, it's not and it doesn't. Illness is not part of the life cycle. The 25th iff December is a false date. We don't have to get or old or infirm, and passion does not have to leave a marriage. It doesn't leave if you're in a sacred union.

Behind Limiting Beliefs

So many people around us are just steps away from being mind controlled bots, or already are. You can recognize them from the glazed stare you receive when bringing up something in the conversation that isn't about makeup or football scores. Common sense says not to engage these individuals directly, as they will robotically repeat MSM hearsay without applying sense or rational function. Some will attack you mercilessly for chinking away at their carefully constructed armor and delusional sense of reality.

Their limiting beliefs are all consuming. Behind these beliefs is fear. This is the fear that you can't do something, or that something outside of you can't be done, or that there isn't some option other than a negative one. Like, *I am going to die from this (fill in the blank) disease.*

Or, *if we have no IRS, then how will taxes be collected and used to support the government?* I have news for these folks. Their taxes aren't being used to support the government. They are being used to pay the Fed for money that we allegedly owe. The Fed is a stand alone entity and not part of our government.

Here's some more on these limiting beliefs, for instance the idea that everyone gets old and sick. I know plenty of people who are moving on in age who are quite healthy and who are in fact quite a bit healthier than many younger people. Likewise, dementia is not a necessary part of aging. It isn't. The toxins in flu shots, environmental poisons, and glucose intolerance is largely responsible for dementia.

What of the limiting belief that if I don't get my children vaccinated, they'll get sick and die? The research of unvaccinated populations is at last surfacing, and populations such as the Amish simply don't experience the illnesses the vaccinated population does. How about my personal favorite, that my friends, church, family, or work associates won't like me anymore if I break out of the social mode of behavior that's accepted by them and start believing things they don't believe. The truth is, most people want to be part of the club.

"The club" is any social group they belong to. It can be a church, a mosque, a temple, their extended family, their neighborhood, the social group at school, the parents of your kids friends. Whatever the group is, they're afraid of being ostracized from it, or looked down upon and somehow challenged if they make the move to leave groupthink.

What's wrong with being challenged? What's behind this? Fear. The fear that others won't like you anymore. Why not just go and start your own club?

Get Rid of Loosh

Death, sadness, despair, anguish...these are things the dark side has perpetrated on humanity since the beginning of time to grow their energetic food supply called loosh. As I've mentioned, this is why wars are created. In addition to creating an immense cash flow wars keep humanity in a perpetual state of fear, anguish and despair.

The dark side grows on these emotions. It helps them become darker, bigger, stronger, and more evil. They are laughing at us and our stupid ability to feel for others. The sooner you accept this, the sooner you will step away from fear or sorrow and go into happy, joyful, abundance.

Love, joy, sharing, unity, peace, faith, hope, joy—this is our natural state. Wars, anguish, and sorrow is an unnatural state that has been perpetrated on us. We have been separated from one another and our true selves on purpose.

Separation leads to loosh. Separation leads to us not loving ourselves, not believing that we're divine, sovereign beings. It's time to accept that we are all one, and we are not creatures of fear.

Chapter 15: Banishing Limiting Beliefs of Yourself & Others

We all know what it's like to be the only one at the dinner table talking about the FDA or the AMA or any of a myriad of things that you know about and they don't. Let's just start with some simple rules on how to finesse this.

Unawake Friends & Family

First of all, no one likes an evangelist. It's not your job to preach. Is it your job to educate? We are presented with a bit of a dilemma because we don't want to be attacked and yet we wish to spread light.

We know that if we do not help facilitate awakening, we're never going to get out of this control system. We walk this careful line of not alienating people and educating at the same time.

So what do we do? The truth is that you really do not have to educate anyone. Your job is to be the light. Embody truth. Be authentic to yourself and your new understandings. Answer truthfully when asked a question, but do not sermonize. Stay detached yet involved. Stay loving yet with boundaries. Your way of being will radiate and affect others just by being you.

But what do you do when you're set on sharing what you've learned after you have received an encouraging flicker of interest?

Sharing Knowledge

Say you're sitting next to someone, or talking with somebody on a call and you realize there's an opening. You're not getting that glazed look, dead silence, or vicious hostility that comes upon people when you mention something outside their realm of understanding. Instead, you're getting a little nod and perhaps even an interested question.

Do not plunge fully in unless invited to do so. Making this mistake will serve to alienate. Believe me, I know. Some of my friends and family think I'm crazy, but most don't because what I've said has been proved right over the years. I've received bumps and bruises along the way and there's no doubt you will as well if you haven't already. So what else do you do?

Keep Emotions Out of It

The most important thing to remember is to never get emotional. This is not about you. This is about changing the game—something far larger than any of us.

If you can speak truthfully with even just one person, imagine how many people they will reach in turn. It's like the old commercial, tell two friends, they tell two friends, and it multiplies exponentially.

Back off from Groupthink

Recognize programming. This is sheeplike groupthink. This is when the other person repeats nonsense because they heard it on the media and are parroting it without any cognitive review. They haven't thought it through yet have accepted it as fact because they heard it from a source they consider an authority, and/or because it's been drummed into their head.

Arguing against programming takes the strength of Job. They will hold on to their false constructs and limiting beliefs for dear life. It's probably best to back off for the sake of your mental health.

Listen

Listen to what the other person is saying. You may not agree with them. It may make your blood boil. You may be saying to yourself, *how can this person be so indoctrinated*, or _____ ? However, if you want them to listen to you, you must listen to them. This is important for your learning. The next time you talk to this individual, you will have more information. For now, hear them out and take mental notes. You're going to encounter this argument again.

If they don't believe what you do, it's okay. It doesn't lessen your value, and it doesn't lessen theirs. It doesn't mean you have to change anything. Maybe the person you are talking with is making valid points. In this case, listen and examine.

Sidestep Tricks

Understand they're going to use cabal tactics on you. They may not be aware of it, but this is what they've been taught. It's part of the indoctrination. Recognize these for what they are: devices and tricks. Real debate has been drummed out of society. Most people are afraid of debate because others don't want their sacred cows challenged. You be the bigger person. Understand that they may be using cabal tactics, but you're not going to do the same. Their techniques include generalizations, repeating hearsay, using illogical reasoning or no reasoning at all, gaslighting, projection, misdirection, and so forth. What do you do about these things? Remain calm. Do not get emotional. This is not about you. This is not an attack on you personally. This is a very big lesson in tolerance for you and quite possibly for the person sitting next to you as well as he or she takes in your calm and authentic demeanor.

This bears repeating: remain calm. Do not get emotional. Do not engage in a fight. Look them in the eye. Let them see how serious, intelligent and focused you are, and that you're not a tinfoil hat wearing lunatic.

You can say something like, *I've put a lot of thought into this. This is not an arbitrary decision on my part. These are just the results of my research and understanding. If you like, we can talk about it. Love you.*

Your Limiting Beliefs

How can you point to the inability of others to take on new information when you may be limiting your own self in this area?

It's important to be vigilant in isolating any lingering limiting beliefs. They usually begin with, *I can't do this.* Or, *if I do this, then this will happen.* If I don't get my kid into the right preschool, then he won't get into the right elementary school, then he won't get into the right junior high, the right high school, the right college, he'll never get a job and he'll have no career!

That's confining you to a box you shouldn't want to be in. One of the forerunners of the truth and disclosure movement, David Icke, says the opposite of fear is unconditional love. At first, I wasn't sure what this meant. Then I thought about it. Fear is low vibration. Unconditional love is high vibration. It's the highest vibration in the universe with the possible exception of authenticity. Those who have been in contact with the galactics say they are fascinated by us because humans experience love in a way that defies their understanding. A high vibration cannot exist with a low vibration in the same body. It just is not possible. One is going to win out over the other. I choose love and hopefully you do too.

Love Yourself

Love yourself and everything around you. This is a great first step. For fear comes from the biggest limiting belief of all, that we are not capable, not in control, not worthy of love, and that we are not the divine sovereign beings we truly are. Those who love themselves and who have begun to love unconditionally know what I am talking about.

Now think about the other low vibration emotions. Hate. Anger. Jealousy. Not only are these emotions feeding the dark side of the planet, but the dark side of your being. These emotions are deteriorating your soul. Imagine giving it all up in favor of unconditional love. The next time someone angers you, put them inside that great big fuzzy heart. Throw in some unicorns and a rainbow or two. Other people have been wounded in their lives just as you have in yours. Maybe they need someone to look up to. It's okay to stand out from the crowd. Maybe they want to follow your lead because inside they know you're right.

Be Aware of Indoctrination

Indoctrination into the commercial society we live in is all around us, everywhere we look. You have to be aware of it to guard against it. Don't say, "Everyone accepts it, so I have to as well." That's no excuse. You can guard against your children seeing inappropriate movies and images by adopting the necessary vigilance. You can monitor them, and when they have experienced something inappropriate for their age range you can explain what it's about. This brings you closer as a parent and helps them understand what they're not supposed to fall prey to in this very adult world. I'll give you an example. A young girl I know was reading an extremely popular teenage book series, that was made into even more popular films.

She was eleven, and when her father become aware of the substance of this book, and that the main character gets pregnant by the end, he got upset and made her stop reading. The young lady was on the last chapter so she became extremely upset herself. She wanted to find out what happened, but the dad explained how he did not want to see her grow up before her time and how these were themes that she was not familiar with yet, and that they needed to talk about them before she heard about them somewhere else. After he explained this to her she turned calm and understanding.

He allowed her to finish that book, but before she proceeded to the next book in the series, she was to give herself time to grow up a little, a few years, actually. She understood his point and agreed. He understood hers. Kids don't need to grow up as quickly as you think they do. They are relieved when you step in as a parent and say, "This is inappropriate." It's not being a prude. At the age of ten or eleven or twelve, do girls and boys really need to think in terms of sex? It's too soon.

Religious Beliefs

This is going to upset a few people so I'm just going to plunge right in. You're still reading so I have to assume that you're at least half believing what I have to say. Religion is contrived to divide us and to take away our divinity as individuals. We are meant to be divine. We were created that way. We are supposed to be one with God.

The evils that have been committed in the name of religion have included some of the worst crimes that have ever been perpetrated on this planet. The Spanish inquisition, Saint Ptolemy's Day, the Holocaust, the Armenian Holocaust, the Serbo-Croatian Holocaust, the Crusades and many more including multiple hidden historical episodes, have been conducted in the name of religion.

This doesn't mean that Judaism or Islam is better than Christianity or any other faith. Islam is responsible for more than a few deaths of their own making. The Ottoman empire rivaled Rome's in brutal destruction. Religion by its nature is meant to separate the individual from the divine. Connection to the divine within is something that must be attained on its own. You do not need to get involved with doctrines and dogma or rituals, priests or rabbis. All that you desire to attain with God can be achieved on your own.

You do not need to be told that you're a sinner. You do not need to be publicly repentant. You do not need to confess your sins to any man or woman. Most priests are fallible in their own right because they are human like the rest of us. Your repentance, if that is what you are called to do, is between you and God, no one else. Take out the middle man. Just as we don't need excessive government, we don't need our personal spirituality in the hands of intermediaries.

Would you put the raising of your child into the hands of somebody else? We have in the schools, unwittingly perhaps. Do you really want to allow somebody else to take over the raising of your child? Don't you want to make your own decisions? Likewise, why would you put your family's spirituality in the hands of someone who isn't you? Religions were created to quash individual power and to keep us from becoming our true, divine, powerful selves.

You, me all of us, are infinitely powerful. A church, mosque, or synagogue may make us feel good and give us the sense of community. There's nothing wrong with that. But when you allow other people to tell you what is divine and what isn't then you are no longer responsible for your divinity and simultaneously you are responsible for all the ills that the church commits in your name. There is only one way to reach divinity, and that is through authenticity and unconditional love.

Upside Down Love

You're told when you're young to grow up and marry someone with money, looks and social status. Everybody is pretty much looking for this "perfection" in a mate. Do we really need the person who is the best income provider or the best social status notch? Or, do we need somebody who is completely in touch with him or herself and who is willing to give himself over one hundred percent to becoming a divine couple with you in God's likeness?

Have you perceived yet that everything in this world is upside down? You will see that very often our standards and goals are not what they should be. As talked about earlier, what's called for is a deep examination of your needs to understand that the person who perhaps has the best career or the best prospects is not necessarily the one who's going to give you the love and the connection that you need.

I'm not talking about people who are completely confused or lost in this world. I'm referring to people who have their head on straight. Be aware that the person who is right for you might not be the one it seems, or that you may have passed over the right one because your goals are not what they should be. What you should be looking for in a mate is the infinite spark, the coming together of two souls who are impossibly attracted to one another, who will grow together, learn together, and love one another unconditionally. Everything can be changed through love.

Chapter 16: Understanding The Dark

An undercurrent of dark worship has infiltrated our planet and is vying for control of our lives. I personally don't know if the pitchfork wielding guy in red exists. What does exist is a contingent of individuals who pursue an antihuman agenda in the dark one's name. As mentioned earlier, whether these individuals are human or reptoid is mostly irrelevant. What is of grave consequence is that a proportion of the population is perpetuating a grave evil that extends to our young people. These individuals do anything for power, greed, to be younger, and to acquire things they value. This comes at the cost of humanity, with the sacrifice of innocence being the highest prize of all.

To me, whether the red guy, or his son, or the goat guy with horns exists, is secondary. The fact that that there are beings who practice things like sex magick and ritualistic sacrifice of our young ones needs to be stopped. If you want to go into depth on this topic I once again point to the docuseries I produced with LifeSource called *Alice In Pedoland*. It is currently on Rumble and links can be found on the LifeSource.global website as well as at the back of this book. The depths to which the dark ones go is beyond human comprehension at times, and this series takes you through gently but thoroughly.

What Are You in Service to?

Jane: It's been suggested that we're looking at 10 to 35% of individuals who worship the dark. A football team took a photo with us in Australia. It was the Aussie Rules grand finals, and three guys at the front of the photo were doing some sort of illuminati symbolism with their hands. It was obvious. I have worked in elite sports for 24 years. Some of my family's best friends are retired elite athletes. My daughter is an elite pro athlete. So I've been around that environment a lot. It's clear to me that there are athletes who are part of the satanic worshipping sect. How did those three in the photo get selected, recruited, brainwashed, manipulated or blackmailed into participating? Why those three and why not the three next to them? This is where I ask, how low down does this go? Because it's in my everyday circle.

Lane: Does this concern you, it being so close?

Jane: It doesn't scare me because we are powerful. It's not an issue. But it interests me. There's a lot of blackmail, obviously. There's a lot of coercion to go into the cults that do evil stuff.

Lane: Satanism is in my opinion, directly connected to hedonism. As we get into a more hedonistic society, the practice of Satanism becomes the quest for the unbridled power they think they can acquire from worship of the occult. This goes back to the black wizard, Alistair Crowley and his teachings. His famous saying is *do as thou wilt*, which means do as you will without repercussions or any morality other than to do what makes you feel good. There's no moral high ground except to serve yourself and whomever you are worshipping in evil's name.

As long as you're doing what you want to do without concern of the harm you are doing to others, you are in service to the dark. To me, those things are grossly connected. Look at all the kids who are being sucked into this because yes, God has left the building, so to speak, with prayer and divinity drummed out of daily life. Our motto in America used to be *in God, we trust*. Now we trust no one.

Jane: Australia was actually founded as an atheistic country.

We were a prison cult, an uncivilized outpost that seemed free but which has actually been under the control of tyrants administering fear. We're seeing the repercussions of that now. One of the reasons we had the most people compliant during Covid was because of fear, fear of death, fear of not following the rules, fear of what the authorities could do to you. There is no spirituality here.

Addressing Evil

Jane: How as a human being do you begin to address this evil? When reacting to this how about saying to yourself, are you coming from fear or are you coming from love?

Lane: That saying has never has resonated with me because I can't understand it on an emotional level. I don't comprehend because I'm always coming from love. I've left fear so far behind I can no longer grasp the feeling. Instead, I say, when you feel fear, you're creating emotional food for them. This is what they want. This is what they feed on. They love when you're distressed or behaving in a hateful way because you are feeding them.

Why would anyone feel hatred? Even in the darkest moments of your life, when people have done you wrong, you shouldn't hate. You might slip and say, I hate you, but you shouldn't feel it. The dark side loves that. They want us to hate each other. *Good*, they think. *They fight each other and not us.*

Becoming Untouchable

To me the more you can go into, I hate to say the cliched, "service to others," but the more you open your heart centers to understand the humanity around you and to allow the love energy to flow through you, to put yourself in others' circumstances and allow yourself to love them, even the most horrible creatures, the higher you will rise. It puts you in a higher state. You become untouchable. This goes back to creating your own reality, the reality your self creates at that level. We are not talking about addressing evil directly here, but how to rise above it, and to keep it from effecting you.

Benevolent Action

Instead of saying service to others, let's say conduct benevolent action. Benevolent action is when you are making sure that every single thing you say and do is not hurtful to someone. Even better than not being hurtful is being helpful in some way. Maybe you're simply serving as a listening device. You know you're there to listen and lend a friendly ear in a supportive way. Maybe you're in a situation where you're being asked to give some direction and guidance.

You don't always know what the other person needs. Maybe they need you to make them understand their self worth, what their unique skills as a human being are. As soon as you start on this, whoever you're talking to will stop and listen. Then they will become rapt as you identify the traits unique or wonderful in them. You focus on that, then from there, it blossoms.

Follow Your Triggers

Jane: You're talking about how to build a deeper connection to others which in turn wards off evil.

Lane: Yes. And in some sense destroys it through starvation. Back to loosh, these negative emotions are not our own. When fear, depression, rage, etc. are created the dark sides sits back and says, *we did this, we created this!*

The whole world is upside down. I think most people have realized that by now. The things that we should love and honor have been inverted and everything that's been told to us is the opposite of truth. Once you realize the world is the opposite of what it should be, it clears up a lot. Understanding the truth of things is an enormous step to eradicating the evil that is all around is. Prayer helps, but sitting in a bubble does not.

Jane: When you are triggered or are feeling that sadness, depression, anger or frustration, in other words lower level emotions, how do you throw them off? How do you raise your vibration?

Lane: Instead of thinking of it as raising your vibration, understand that it's the byproduct, a damn good byproduct, of flipping things around. Following our triggers is the path to self realization and ascendency. We're still working on them because they happen so quickly and seemingly out of nowhere, just like that game where you smash the frogs with a mallet as they pop up. When we think we're through another one shows up, and bam! You follow it. Sadness, frustration depression, etc., once you recognize them, can be flipped around.

Now, of course, I don't have a chemical imbalance. Perhaps this is because I take care of myself in a very natural, holistic way. If you have a physical issue it may not be so easy at the start. Go back to the chapter on physical health and eliminate stressors. You've got to work it through.

I don't get depressed, not anymore, but move back 30 years when I was being rejected by publishers and not getting my work looked at, I would get depressed over each rejection letter. I would go into my bed and pull the covers over my head and sleep. Sometimes I needed five minutes, sometimes longer. My secret weapon against depression was sleep, always. It is as of the act of turning off your mind allows you to bypass unproductive thoughts and focus on what counts. Your thoughts become clear and unjumbled. Ask for Source to step in and help with this. Sleep will turn around a depression especially if you ask for help. I'd come out of it feeling better. I think my spirit angels were saying while I snoozed, *Oh, you're fine. You can wake up now.*

The upshot of this experience was unbreakable self knowledge and self worth. Eventually, I no longer needed to be validated from outside sources. I was very grateful for that experience. Even as it was happening, I was understanding it. I kept writing until I was such a good writer that no one could break me. This extended over a ten year period and while it was awful to go through, it brought me to new heights of skill and empowerment.

Depression, sadness, frustration—all are there for a reason. That adage is a universal truth. Everything has a reason. Everything *does* have a reason. Follow this to its source.

Flip the Program

Sometimes you can figure out the reason for your triggers

easily. Sometimes you have to meditate on it or think it through, and as I said, ask your guides for a greater understanding of it. Sometimes it takes a lifetime to figure things out. Everything you experience is part of your path.

The obstacles are opportunities. Frustration should disappear with the knowledge that this is a learning experience. Don't be so hard on yourself. Sadness is a hard one if you've lost somebody, but also know that there's no such thing as death, and that they remain right there with us, for as long as we need them.

Government Sponsored Mind Control

At the risk of this coming off like a sci-fi script, I am going to share some details regarding one of the government's most evil and pervasive operations. I heavily debated whether to leave this part out, but in the end decided I needed to provide an overview.

MKUltra is a mind control program developed in the 1950s by the CIA, which has Satanic ritual abuse (SRA) at its core. This is part of the bloodline rituals I mentioned earlier. The program is heavily in use despite official denials, and is being practiced more so now than ever.

This kind of abuse is deeply tied to a satanic agenda and underlies all aspects of global dominance, including corporate hegemony, medical tyranny, and manipulations of human emotions, cognition, freedom and rights.

MKUltra is a system of controlling brain patterns, personality, and an individual's innate morality, impelling that person to commit unnatural, deviant acts, that if left to their own devices, they would never commit.

The horrendous abuse suffered by victims of MKUltra is quite literally soul shattering. Ritualized, torturous punishments beginning during gestation and continuing through infancy, childhood, and into adulthood, fracture the mind and cause the personality to dissociate. This creates what is called Dissociative Identity Disorder, or DID. These personalities are distinct entities whose memories and skills separate from one another while operating under the mantle of a single host being.

You might have a person whose name is Kim. Kim's true personality recedes into the background while Sam, Harry, Elizabeth, Mandy, and Pippi become her dissociative personalities. Kim may be so far gone into the background that she disappears, quite possibly forever.

The varying personalities are called upon as needed for specific functions via a pre-programmed trigger. For instance Sam comes forward when a boyish looking female is needed for sex acts. Pippi appears for perverse acts that extend beyond the realm of what normal individuals can withstand. Some are programmed as "presidential models" and trained as honeypots. Some are designed to infiltrate public thinking in the media. Most MKUltra victims are groomed to be highly intelligent. Some are programmed for performance in the music and entertainment industries and are used to over sexualize kids. Some are programmed to kill.

SRA training starts with parents who are very often mind controlled themselves. There are handlers within the CIA community who are activated at key moments during the individual's life in order to take the training to new levels. Some of these handlers stay by the slave's side throughout their lifetime.

For these programmed individuals are in essence, slaves. They've lost the connection to their humanity, free will, and any ability to lead purposeful, authentic lives.

MKUltra mind control programming is practiced within bloodline families who pass the tradition from generation to generation. The practice is not in anyway limited to them, as innocent children from all walks of life are used for programmed functions, as well as for sacrifice and rituals. Often the children of pedophiles, rapists, or criminals are used and discarded. These are occult throwaways.

Books by reputable sources are easily found and downloadable on the internet. There's plenty of information out there. On social media you'll find survivors identifying their abusers and speaking out as their memories return. Their stories are heartrending as they share the arduous process of reintegrating their dissociative beings.

Types of MKUltra Programming

There are multiple types of slaves. Some alters are programmed as intelligence assets or spies, assassins, military strategists, combat soldiers, martial arts experts, or weapons experts. One of the most common is called Beta, or Monarch programming.

These are sex weapons. Boys, girls, men, and women are used to influence through media, television, film, music, and so on. Let's not forget the presidential model Marilyn Monroe, who was a throwaway.

Many people are now aware of the Satanic element within entertainment, music and sports if not yet fully recognizing what they are: mass programming rituals being perpetrated on the public. Indications that a ritual is taking place include the presence of goats or horns representing Baphomet, triangles, one eye, and in general, dark or upsetting performances. The use of black and white, which symbolizes mind dissociation, and surrealist distortion techniques are often used.

How MKUltra Programming Works

In its extreme form MKUltra programming involves sadistic, cruel, and inhumane forms of behavior modification in order to get desired results.

A mind controlled slave can be designed to do anything. In order to create this situation, a set of events must occur that reverse the natural instincts of right versus wrong, and concepts of good versus evil. In other words, MKUltra Programming reverses our innate state of goodness, mercy, and love while making the inverse true instead. The program is that harming others is good and worthy of reward, in essence, turning everything that is good upside down.

In its extreme, when the torture becomes too much to bear, the personality splits off and creates an altar, or another personality. This process is continued until hundreds of altars are created in a single being. Severe forms of torture are used to get a young soul to override every natural instinct it has been bestowed with, such as trusting parents, expecting a mother's love, and being rewarded for being good. The personalities are taught to mistrust tenderness, affection, love from other humans. Instead, a reverse system is put into operation. Here painful consequences are imposed for natural behavior and rewards imposed for unnatural behavior. In this way a system of action is created much like Pavlov's dog, wherein the splintered personalities are rewarded for acting in the way the controllers dictate.

How This Affects Us

You may be thinking that while this program is indeed terrible, it has little to do with you. Unfortunately, this could not be further from the truth. Widespread trauma programming is very real and is present in every moment of our lives by design. 9-11 was a mass trauma programming event. So is every shooting, accident or tragedy. When our emotions are laid bare our susceptibility to programming increases. While the ability to feel for others is one of our greatest strengths, it has also been recognized by the dark side as our greatest weakness and their best opportunity. They have deliberately used this tactic on us at every juncture. What is the solution? Not to stop feeling, but to realize that excessive mourning, depression, despair, or rage, and so on, leaves you vulnerable to being programmed in a way that will counter your most innate sense of right and wrong and erode your unalienable right of personal sovereignty. Be aware, and don't let this happen to you.

Chapter 17: Avoiding Further Traps

Living in an inversion of that which grows the human spirit and instead moves us into a negative state keeps us in dense 3D vibration. How do you escape this when surrounded by evils of the most horrendous kinds?

People are of the opinion that humans are aggressive in nature, but we are not. Left to our own devices we love each other, we marry each other, we have babies with one other, we invite each other over for picnics, and we watch out for the children no matter who they belong to.

Every division, attempted annihilation, and war we've experienced has been fabricated by those who wish us harm. They do this by creating the perfect situation for discord.

Emotional Manipulation

Sometimes we have to go back in time in order to perceive how we've been manipulated. Then we can move forward in an unprogrammed way. Look at the Israeli Palestinian conflict. This is an example of a war being fought in the headlines.

They have been doing this blatant manipulation for decades, in which they fool the public into believing that someone is under attack and needs to be saved. I don't know how much of what we're seeing now is legitimate. I would guess very little. Much of the "news" being shown to the public is fabricated, old or photoshopped. Some may remember the Iraqi girl, Nayirah al-Ṣabaḥ, who talked about Kuwaiti babies being pulled from their incubators by Iraqi soldiers, The public outrage helped kick off the Gulf War. It was later revealed that she was the ambassador's daughter, and she'd been set up to manipulate public opinion. The use of children is an old one. They have paraded them before us to kick off world wars, and have even done so with the false concept of climate change. The film *Wag the Dog* explains the process perfectly, and should be watched as a documentary.

They have to make every conflict seem as real as possible. They love bloodshed and carnage because as we've said, it lowers our vibration while feeding theirs. By now people should understand that the lower our vibration goes, the more energy it generates for the dark side. Withholding their energy is a powerful way to fight back.

When we see these images and worry that we're going to be bombed or receive terror attacks, know that's exactly how they want us to feel. We have contingents of refugees in all of our countries now, potentially consisting of standing armies of fighting age men who have been given smartphones and envelopes filled with cash. Are they going to be activated? The situation for division, turmoil and fear has been adroitly created. The trick is to feel no fear while taking positive, peaceful and proactive action.

Energetic Leaning

Honest debate could start to get us to truth, but our soul's advancement can get us there more rapidly when we lean into the energy of the situation. That means learning to trust yourself and your instincts.

This instinctual knowing leads us into deep discernment, an empowered combination of head and heart. You can lean into a situation energetically and feel the truth of it. To do this properly you have to first shut out the outside noise, including most importantly, the lies, propaganda and emotions of others. Remove all emotion and look at the situation objectively.

How do we do this when the news has fighting on all sides with people shouting death threats while waving photos of dead grandmothers? How do you separate yourself emotionally?

Being Objective

As events increase in severity, we're being asked to develop at a faster rate. This is an opportunity for your soul's growth. Let's go back to that war in Yugoslavia, which serves as an example of how war was created where there didn't need to be one.

If you, the globalist, knew that a certain people had experienced annihilation at the hands of their fascist-controlled brethren four decades previously, then it does not take much to rekindle that memory and fear. In the ensuing rush to take up arms in protection of their loved ones, this group becomes the aggressor in the press, a situation which spirals out of control by design. This enables the globalist and his friends to bomb the heck out of these people and cow what was once a proud nation into submission. You can then take control of their homeland which is rich in oils and precious minerals. You can also set up the largest military base in the world in their disputed territory.

Something similar is happening with the Jews and Palestinians. A new trade route is being created while the world focuses on the fake atrocities being presented in the news. What is the truth? Follow the money. The Hamas is bought and sold. So is Netanyahu. We gave them both money. We gave Iran money and left our equipment in Afghanistan for terrorists to use. We have fomented horrible feeling against the West among the Muslim populations of the world. Look at those who are in our countries now. They hate us. They don't want to be American, British or Australian, necessarily, even though they're here with their hands out.

The hatred is created. What's involved here is stepping away and becoming objective. We are members of the same human family and have got to find a way to put aside our differences. Humanity is at a crossroads. The time has come for us to stop allowing our thoughts and actions to be manipulated and to stand together as one. There is no other choice.

Stagnation is No Option

Where does that leave us? You've got to rise. Don't take the bait and instead rise to your highest, most divine level. That's what's being asked of us as humanity. The pain and suffering is being ratcheted up. Why? From a spiritual level, you're being asked to grow into who you really are. Otherwise the situation will get worse. That's karma, remember? Learn your lesson on the spot and the karma will go away.

Will we make it? It depends on whether "we" means all of us or some of us. I don't know if everyone's going to be able to do this. Will they suffer as a result? I don't know. I only know the lessons are going to get more and more severe until something gives.

Avoiding Traps

Respect the laws of karma. We've talked about this: If you don't learn your lessons and grow from the experience, the karma is going to get progressively harder. Because the purpose is to grow and to learn and not fall prey to all the side traps along the way that include the corruption of power, money, greed, and ego.

All those are traps. So is war. So is hating your neighbor. That's a huge trap. The task is to sidestep the traps and grow.

Jane: Both sides of the camp have fallen hook, line and sinker for the divide and conquer trap. They have fallen right into it and are contributing to the conflict by fanning the flames. The dark side is adept at understanding what the triggers of each culture are.

I think you are 100 percent right. That we're spiritually being asked to level up, to grow, to rise above, to sidestep the trap.

Lane: They know the triggers for each of us, and that gets us attacking one another.

Jane: Absolutely. They created the program. They started the whole thing.

Lane: We love each other. That's our natural state of being.

They created a program to make us believe that we're warlike and hateful.

Jane: That's mirroring what the bad side is, meaning those who wish to harm us. So that's the intention.

Lane: I always fall back to the Hitler argument where some say it initiated rapidfire spiritual growth that allowed a massive amount of karma to be worked through at once. I don't know the answer to this, but I do know that in every situation there's good and bad.

Jane: On a certain level it's all about contrast. Without contrast, we don't have awareness. Without contrast we're on a hilltop eating mung beans, watching the sun rise, no expansion, and we're complacent. We came here for a vibrational conscious awareness experience, which is only created through contrast.

Lane: I believe also we've come here to grow into our divinity and our oneness with the Creator, or the creative element.

Jane: You can't do that without an emotional barometer. And an emotional barometer is only activated by observation of what is. Each of us has the ability to create our own reality by observing what is.

Lane: We do create our own reality, and this is where it always gets layered, as in *whoa, wait! How many realities are there*? Infinite, in my opinion. I once found that confusing, the idea that we create our own reality. Now I'm a believer. I've experienced too much not to wholeheartedly believe in manifestation and reality creation. Yet while we create a good reality on a certain level, meaning those of us who are aware and who are working on it, what about those stuck in a warfare situation?

I don't want to be part of it, but what if my neighbor is slain? Then you're part of it. That's the challenge, isn't it? What role are we going to play? How are we going to show up? What is our reaction?

Jane: Are we coming from love or are we coming from fear? And it's okay to feel angry as long as it doesn't take over you.

Lane: Yes, absolutely as long as you work through it. Does that give rise to new awareness? Yes. Can that give rise to changed reactions? Yes. Can that give rise to action that leads to change? Yes.

Jane: That's right. In self and community and collective consciousness.

Lane: So a reality is not necessarily the circumstance. It's how you react to the circumstance.

Jane: That's a reality. Perfectly said.

Lane: Then there's the reality of not participating in a lot of this garbage that goes on every day.

Jane: That's an interesting question because early in 2020 I had a lot of spiritual friends who said, I don't care about this Covid thing.

I'm thinking, I'm fighting an energetic war here 24/7 and you just want to go drink your lattes by the beach. I was furious and said, *we need you*. You're aware of all of this agenda. We need boots on the ground. But then I realized there are many roles to be played in this.

Lane: Roles by those who can hold a vibration of peace, unity, and oneness.

Jane: Those are the people laying the grids or contributing to the grid lines.

Lane: A lot lack courage and direction. As you say, they have spiritually bypassed. That's where it comes back to the individual and what they choose.

Jane: Where were they in their growth? I had to learn to accept where they were. But I didn't want to hear their lectures about how it was a set up. My inner child got very triggered at that.

Group Karma

The Covid situation is the perfect example of all of us having to live through group karma. For some it's been harsher than others. Like every other major event, people who refuse to open their eyes to see what's going on or who lack the moral courage to take a stand have felt the sand shift under their feet. In other words, their secure place within the world, no matter what place they are at, becomes threatened. If you go back to the American Revolution, you knew that if you spoke up you were taking your life in your hands. There are a number of people in this movement today, the one for humanity's freedom, who have had to make a choice as to whether they were willing to forfeit their life if necessary.

A lot of us made that decision and that's what's called for here. Even young parents with children need the moral courage to step up and make noise when things are bad. You need to pick your role, choose your side.

Jane: Let's talk about that. Pick your roles because as you were speaking I was envisaging that everybody can step up. Now, you don't have to step up and be a bold warrior like those putting their names and likenesses on truth documentaries about dangerous subjects.

Lane: You don't have to be like the doctors who are giving up their licenses rather than treat people with a poisonous jab, who opt for delivering truth over AMA lies. You don't have to be like the whistleblowers who are speaking about transhumanism and us being wired to some sort of groupthink, also putting their lives on the line. People don't have to do that. But a concrete decision has to be made. Which side are you on? Because sitting on the sidelines drinking lattes no longer cuts it.

We should all have metaphorical pitchforks in our hands. We can't let these government actors continue doing what they're doing. It's going to get increasingly difficult for us until we stop them. Those beings are not our governors. We're under siege.

Yes, we're in a war, not just spiritual war, but a physical one as well. We are 100% occupied. Most every country is. People just don't realize the depth of it because they can't accept that people can actually be as bad as they are. But these are not people. They are not human. If they were human at one time they long ago lost the capacity for love and compassion.

Phase III: Our Best Selves

"Nietzsche was the one who did the job for me.
At a certain moment in his life, the idea came to him of what he called 'the love of your fate.'
Whatever your fate is, whatever the hell happens, you say, 'This is what I need.' It may look like a wreck, but go at it as though it were an opportunity, a challenge. If you bring love to that moment—not discouragement—you will find the strength is there."
Joseph Campbell on Socrates and the Unexamined Life

Chapter 18: Incoming Abundance

Once you accept the fact that coincidences don't exist an inner shift occurs. There was a term I remember from a TV show called Family Ties. Alan Thicke's character always used the word *coincidink*. It formed the phrase that runs through my head: *No such thing as coincidink*. Once I took the concept of everything being intentional on one level or another, meaning by spiritual design, I saw the significance in everything.

Making Connections

Take a look at sacred geometry. The forms and ratios are echoed in every live thing on this planet, within the planet itself, and within our very cells. Whether it's a cell network of an oak leaf, the pattern on a turtle shell, a nucleic cluster, or a junction of synapses, all forms of life repeat the same sacred geometry forms. How is that random? It's not. It's by design and not a coincidence.

If you accept that every single thing you run across in the course of your day has significance, then you'll start to see the connections between things. You'll start to see the patterns in ways that make sense, and you'll start to get messages. With this comes the glorious enjoyment of the beauty in all things.

Numbers and Other Signs

Soon the signs become clear and easier to follow. You can get to a point where you see messages everywhere. Numbers on license plates make sense, as numerology pops up. This is the reduction of every number and letter to 1 through 9, adding them up and reducing them again. I don't have to be told when I'm in a nine phase. I know it because everything is coming out to a nine. A nine phase is of a philosophical bent and signals the end of a cycle. It means you're moving on. In the most simple terms, one is the beginning of a cycle. It indicates leadership and forging ahead. Two is community. Three is creativity, four is endeavor, five is public attention, six is family, seven is spirituality, and eight is abundance. Tomes have been written that explore this in depth. In fact, my own parents wrote *The Book on Numerology*. Take a look for it. It's by Joyce and Jack Keller.

Numbers have patterns and meaning that go deeply into the mysteries of life. 3, 6, and 9 particularly, hold the secret to the universe according to the great Nikola Tesla. In fact, Tesla realized this was the key to manifestation, a process I lay out for you in both my emotional healing cards and manifestation calendar. See the back pages for more on this.

Astrology

If you follow astrology you will note there is an overlap between numbers and planet placements. Some don't give importance to astrology, and especially horoscopes, and in truth much of it is wrong. This is partly because astrology needs intuitive interpretation and the whole birth chart must be taken into account not just the sun sign. If you take in the entirety of where the planets were and their conjunctions with one another at the time and place of your birth, you'll get an entirely different picture.

Astrology and numerology support one another. That synchronicity to me signals a universe by design. You may question how much free will we actually have in the case of astrological or numerological predictions, but these practices are indicators of the being you incarnated into at birth. They are signposts, if you will, providing a blueprint with pitfalls to avoid and highs to enjoy. You are at liberty to study this blueprint as part of your self realization process in which you come to understand yourself better but by no means is it a pronouncement.

You don't not have to follow this program, or any other. As a means of isolating tendencies and things to watch out for, both astrology and numerology can be a great help. Anything can be of help in the hands of a truly intuitive individual, whether it's reading tea leaves or the phases of the moon. Every once in a while, when I pay attention to the interpretation of lunar phases, I think *wow, that's so accurate.*

People who work in the health fields will tell you the full moon means something for sure. More accidents happen around eclipses than at any other time of the year. Is this divine design? I have observed that big things happen on eclipses. Truly gifted interpreters will expose a world of understanding of you open yourself to it.

Karma and Free Will Interaction

The idea of free will is that you make your own choices and determine your own fate. You can't impose on another's will because they will be experiencing the effects and repercussions and not you. Of course you can experience repercussions for impinging on somebody's free will, which is the result of your own action.

Whatever someone does is going to generate a balancing effect or lesson, whether good, bad, or neither. Let them experience it because it's going to hopefully bring them to a higher level. I hope that the people I love don't suffer ill effects from making certain choices. If they do, I have to accept that as part of their lesson in this life. If you choose to ignore the repercussions of your actions, karma becomes more severe. It's just the way it works. So make those free will choices in alignment with the highest good for all, but not sacrificing yourself in the process.

Frequency Manipulation

People in this movement send out manipulations of frequencies. I don't think it's wrong to send out positive vibrations, but you need to be up front about what you are putting out there. What is very wrong is to send out subliminal messaging if you don't inform those listening. This is a cabal technique and is brainwashing under a different name.

I feel that we have lost a lot of our free will. Humanity is not acting in 100 percent free will capacity because of the mind control sickness that's been imposed on us, the consistent use of frequency, and continual, blatant programming. I feel that as a whole we are operating at about 4 percent level of free will. Eliminate the programming and your ability to act in accordance with your own free will skyrockets.

Consent

Free will is impaired when you don't have all the information, which is maybe why I am dead set on ascertaining bottom line truth. Without that, we cannot act fully in our own authenticity of our own accord. We're all doing the best we can while flying into a thunderstorm in the night with a console board that's gone dark. Most of us are acting without the correct information to make proper decisions.

Missing Information

You might think vaccines are good because you believe your doctor when he says long term testing has been done. But he leaves out the fact that the long term testing was not done on humans, or with the correct dosages, or with the proper control groups. How many parents make decisions with faulty information? While it falls on all of us to do proper research, Google and mainstream sources are corrupt. They have so hidden the truth that it takes real detective skill to find accurate answers.

Consent is of great importance and we are giving it without having the facts. Additionally we are not asked to give our consent for a lot of what we've experienced on this planet, and likewise some has happened before we were born where we signed onto contracts of which we have no cognitive memory in this lifetime. Not as of yet. This lack of knowledge refutes consent. I personally cannot consent to something I can't remember. So either give me the memory of it or I refute it. I don't know what aspects I entered into until I have cognition of that, and I don't acknowledge them. They have no power over me.

I do not give my consent. I especially refute any and all spells or negativities that may have been imposed on me or my loved ones. I do not consent. You have to be very careful of the things to which you consent. Just by being quiet you've given your agreement. Silence is consent.

Jane: You've given your tacit agreement to something because you haven't explored it properly. You don't understand it, and you've given somebody else power over you, and that is unacceptable.

Lane: Completely unacceptable. Worse yet, you're affecting your children's lives because of your lack of knowledge and your tacit consent. I think a lot of people know now about the agreement those working in the dark have made. This agreement states that they can perpetuate their negative crap on us as long as they let us know what they're doing. This is supposed to lessen any repercussions they may receive from the Lords of Karma, or whatever they believe in.

They're very sly and have swept all sorts of information into subtle forms of disclosure. Many people are now aware of the predictive programming coming through sources like the Simpsons. Matt Groening, the Simpsons' creator is worth 500 million dollars and is part of the Hollywood club. Aldous Huxley who wrote the prophetic *Brave New World* in 1939, predicted the world we live in today with amazing accuracy. He and his protégé, George Orwell, who wrote the seemingly prophetic *1984*, were part of the Fabian Society where they learned of the plans of the totalitarian order firsthand. With the blessing, or perhaps instruction, of higher ups they disclosed these plans in the form of fiction.

The Illuminati card deck is another form of disclosure, telling us everything they are doing in the form of playing cards. The accuracy in which they depict future events would seem uncanny if you didn't know that their creators were simply privy to the plans for humanity. There is great importance behind these information leaks. In the controllers' opinion, by us not saying *no*, we have consented to this plan for us. In their opinion we have agreed. So say *no*! Make noise. Say aloud, *I do not consent!* There is much being exposed every day in films and TV shows. Look though the veils of secrecy and see the truth.

Language

Some people think that the use of proper speech and grammar is elitist, but I think not. Unable to understand language and grammar is exactly how they want us to be: dumbed down, unable to fully communicate, only able to talk in broad terms without nuanced detail. What does that sound like? A caveman. The more command we have over our individual languages and vocabulary, the more intricately we can express ourselves and our ideas. Thus, the more we can advance ourselves. This is not to avoid the fact that language has been deliberately skewed to keep us in a low vibrational limited state. As we evolve higher, spoken words will become less necessary as we telepathically communicate ideas to one another, however complex, in a single thought.

This is not to ignore the whole issue of *spelling*, in which letters have been switched around and in many cases inverted to create a spell of which we are fully unaware. This is another one of the Cabal's little tricks. The word spelling itself is the perfect example in which SPELL -ing demonstrates the meaning of letter placement. We can combat this by imbuing our thoughts and words with positive intent.

You see, it all comes down to inverting all the negativity that has been imposed on us. Once you recognize it, it's easy to do with everything you see, say, or encounter.

Regarding the lessening of standards we consider civilized, do we really want to go back to caveman time? Because that's what they'd love to have happen. Holding a door open or a pulling out the seat for a woman is not elitism or a display of toxic masculinity. It is a sign of respect that says, *I value you*. These little courtesies have been largely eliminated from our society as we grow increasingly unpleasant towards one another.

The elitist use manners to mask their hypocrisy and are the opposite of what they pretend. They're demonic vampires who embody every bad thing you can think of. They use language and fake courtesy against us. But we can use language against them by fully expressing ourselves and learning to communicate telepathically, which happens naturally as we vibrate higher.

Self-education is a big part of this. Libraries and free pdfs on the net are still available to us, which hold the philosophers, the Greeks, the Egyptians, and tomes of wisdom including the mystery schools, if you dig hard enough.

We've lost the skill, I know I have, of understanding old and archaic wording. Although it's difficult to make it through, we want that wisdom, without an interpreter or guide if possible. Eventually we will get to the point where everything we want to access will be available by simply pulling it down from the ethers.

Your Unknown Superpower

There is much talk of humanity moving into crystalline, higher frequency physical bodies. I think that is certainly plausible, but I don't know this with certainty. I do know that there are waves of incoming energy that can bring you up or bring you down and flatten you out.

Jane: When I tap into your energy, I don't have any concerns for you. None at all. I say though, will you just eff-ing rest? That's what I get.

Lane: I'm challenging the narratives, the programs that we've got. I'm asking, is there a different way other than a continual outpouring of energy?

Jane: You resting is bothering you because mentally you're feeling you're not achieving, not striving. We've got the world to save.

Lane: It's just that I have a to do list I can't even get near. So I started back up in this exercise class. It's not hyper crazy. Yet I can sometimes barely move my body. That's how bad it gets sometimes. Everyone else is jumping around saying, *this is great! I'm so energized. I feel wonderful,* while I'm thinking, *Oh my gosh. Get me to bed.* These are the phases in which I feel completely drained. They don't last long and seem to be cyclical but they do come without warning.

Jane: I've had a lot of periods like that over the years, a lot. I actually did a podcast on what we feel is laziness years ago. Everybody needs permission to be so called, lazy. Because again, that's just a program.

The cohost on that particular show was a psychic medium. Her channeling on laziness say it has to do with spiritual connection, spending more time on rest, giving ourselves permission to stare into space, and so on. This is when souls actually hop out of the body and go on a little adventure.

Lane: For all we know, people wanting to rest, lie down, and sleep is your soul saying, *all right, I've got to go and gather some more information. I'm going over to another galaxy and check out that and I'll come back with more info.*

Jane: Do you remember in Avatar where they plug in to their conscious thing and take the consciousness out of the body and put it into the big avatars?

Lane. Yes. What a great movie.

Jane: If we were observing those people in the flesh, you'd think they're sleeping. I actually suspect that sleep is where our greatest activity occurs. It makes sense to me that there would be a program from Deep State around sleep where they give us drugs to sleep to stop all of the activity that would be happening otherwise.

Lane: They make sure that we've got electronic devices next to us when we're sleeping. They do so much to disrupt our sleep including mucking around with daylight savings times and having us work and not have enough holidays. All of that is to ensure our sleep isn't the quality it should be, because that's where life actually really happens.

When I have to process material, because it's difficult or requires a different part of my brain to understand, I go to sleep. If I've had an emotionally jarring experience I process it through sleep as well, in as little as 30 seconds. Then it's like, *Poof! All better. All is clear now.*

Jane: I don't have them very often now, but when I used to have an upset I would go straight to sleep to rebalance my body. I think that here we've just flipped a narrative. Sleep is a superpower that they don't want us to know about.

Lane: We have to change our expectation of what achievement is. We're a bit addicted to getting things done, but listening to your body and saying, *Yep, I'm going to sleep and I'm not going to get concerned,* is crucial.

Jane: It doesn't matter if I'm not paying the bills or writing the next great documentary. As long as the electricity is not getting turned off it's fine. Just don't let the Wi Fi turn off.

Lane: Exactly.

Jane: Priorities. So because you're in a tired state. You might find it's quite interesting what comes through today for you with the book.

Chapter 19: Personal Spirituality

Many people ask what spirituality is and the answer varies. Understanding and developing your own relationship with the Divine, in whatever form that takes for you is your personal spirituality.

I recently went on an outing with a friend who brought along an acquaintance of his. Before we met my friend said, "You're going to love him. He's very spiritual." When I met this individual he gave me an immediate rundown of the church he ran before then asking, what church do you go to? In other words, *where do you go to be spiritual?* Taken aback I answered, "the church of me and God."

What did he mean, what church do I go to? I pondered this. I don't go to any physical church. I don't have any barrier between me and God. That was my initial reaction and perhaps I was triggered because I had expected someone beyond this. It was by way of a reminder that some people still think spirituality means going to church.

I do believe spirituality is having a direct connection between yourself and divinity, whatever form that divinity takes. This might be the Creator God, Mother God, Father God, Source, the Universe, and so on. Some say there is more than one god, that there are many, and that they're under the master God. The female aspect of God I believe is one with male. To me God is neither gender.

Spirituality is tapping into your highest, best self using a developed sense of intuition and discernment. You go to the heart to work on the development of your inner self and in so doing, get closer to a state of divinity. Spirituality is the quest for personal divinity. What's at the other end of that is us becoming god creators. This is not to usurp God's position or to say that we are on the level of God. But we are going to grow in Source light ourselves and merge with the true, larger Source. What we will find on the other end of this journey is that we are all the same, and are all divine aspects of one another.

The Ascended State of Being

To me the dimensions, or the steps up the ascension ladder represent our state of being in a given moment. The ascension process is growing into a greater awareness of yourself and others and how you fit into this whole. This occurs as you move through the dense 3D material world and into the higher realms, where things become energetic.

I can't say for certain what lies beyond the fifth dimension. I have heard various scenarios, but I have not personally experienced them in this life as far as I know. I would say it's a totally beautiful and a bliss like state where we are what we were meant to be, which are beautiful loving creatures.

Mark Twain told the tale of the fire ants in one of his short stories. He said if you put red and white fire ants together in a jar and close the lid they're perfectly happy and they work together. But if you shake the jar, the ants will start attacking one another. Our true state is a loving embracing state where things move energetically. That to me is what at least the start of what fifth dimension is all about.

5D is a higher state of divinity. It is the gateway to 6D and beyond. Here you lose the ego and are no longer in it for just yourself or your family. You're in it for the greater good. You're in this whole thing, whatever this is, together, as we exist in a beautiful giving state.

We should never believe something that we're told. We always need to search for the truth so as to feel into it ourselves, using a combination of intellect or intuition. When I am researching a historical time period I need to keep digging and digging because the historical through line has been so violently distorted. I don't go by what I have been told or what I hear without taking all viewpoints into consideration. The viewpoint of those who have lived through a given event will vary greatly from person to person, even those who are on the same alleged side. Finding the commonality is how I bring things down to an empirical, bottom line truth, or as best I can ascertain what that truth is.

A Grain of Salt

Everything, whether it's coming from the spirit world, a trusted psychic, an "authority," guru or leader of some sort, must be taken with a grain of salt, in other words, it must be deeply examined through a discerning lens.

Those who've worked on this for a long time can feel things energetically. We can feel the energy of something and whether or not it seems correct. If not getting something immediately we can take a step back and do an energetic read and go so far as to say, *I'm going to give that one a 70% on the truth scale.*

I know that if something doesn't resonate, or in another way of putting it, vibrates at a frequency incongruent with myself, I back off from that source of information. Most often what happens is we've got a mixture of truth with falsehood and we particularly find that is the case in the "truth movement" where information has become increasingly distorted. It's catching up to mainstream media, which has up to this point been 99.999% distorted.

There's much disinfo flying around in the form of false throughlines and narratives. When all of this is said and done, meaning the moment in time when the inhabitants of earth at last throw off the shackles and emerge as our truly loving and authentic selves, we're going to look back at the various throughlines and hopefully laugh, and say, *I can't believe I fell for that!*

We need to be on guard constantly to learn what the truth actually is. If a piece of information has some seeming truth I hold on to it and like I shared earlier, I say, o*kay, that could be until I can rule it out.*

This is true with the endless debates on things like flat earth. There's a lot of credibility on both sides, and also a lack of credibility on both sides. If you listen to the arguments you'll either find them fascinating, worthy of tin foil, or a complete time waster. The one thing for certain is that we don't have enough info. I don't think that the truth has yet been revealed on this issue.

I will say this. I was given an image of the earth, clairvoyantly, which you can find in my bear book, *A Tale of Running Bear*, published by Arelian Press. The link is included at the end of this book. This is a storybook I created, which was given to me word for word by a visiting bear. I can't say how or why that transpired, only that I was very grateful for the experience. This image coincided with what the earth dome theorists are describing and I hold it as a distinct possibility.

The point is that nothing should be accepted outright. If you examine your belief structures, and as discussed we have very many of them, you'll know the history that we were taught in school and books is false.

There's so much falsity around us that everything has to be put under the microscope. Most people don't want to do this. They want to live their lives in peace and take things as they come. They hear it on the news, or pronounced by some authority figure and they accept it. They don't examine it, and they don't subject it to research. There's no desire to get down to the real truth of things and that is pretty alarming.

Jane: Do you think that's because they're worn out from a system that is designed to exhaust them?

Lane: I don't think exhaustion is the word. I think they're distracted. They're distracted by day jobs. They're distracted by being the perfect mother or parent. You have this high level expectation of what parenting and the perfect life entails. Your friends, your social circle—it takes work to keep up with that.

Bringing your kids to schools and ball games and ballet lessons is a ton of work. Then you get home and prepare a meal, with baths, homework, stories and bedtime, and yes, you are exhausted. You're going to pass out on the couch and watch idiotic TV until you fall asleep.

Then there's the financial trap of people having to have two jobs in order to pay mortgages and bills with the cost of living still going up. There's the Joneses where you have to have the right house and the right car in the right neighborhood so your kids can go to the right school and associate with the right people. Where is the focus on what is important? Do they need to wait for something to rattle their cage?

About Loved Ones

There are many theories about where the earth is going in this spiritual ascendance we are undergoing. Some, such as interdimensional experiencer Alex Collier, who relays information from the Andromedans, say the earth itself is moving into 4D. Collier also relays that some of us didn't necessarily rise to 5D but instead arrived here as 5D. We actually came here as 11D, then through the process of the densities of earth, got funneled down to 5D.

According to this theory, those who are of a lower dimension than four are not going to be able to come on board. In 2012, there was to be a dimensional shift where the planet was going to split. Dolores Cannon talks about two earths. Others talk about the fifth dimension splitting off from the earth, as in: *pack your etheric suitcase, we're out of here.* Then of course are the various exodus theories, where we need tickets to leave on some given spaceship. My own supposition came down to different dimensions living alongside one another on planet earth. As your vibration rose you could perceive the other dimensions. If you were of dense vibration you could not, and would believe that you were alone.

What I do know is that not everyone is developing at the same rate and that there has been an ongoing shift. I've wondered what was going to transpire. Are some of us leaving and others staying? Both the suitcase and spaceship theories have some staying behind. As the years pass, I see us toiling to rise up, to educate, to uplift, and revibrate humanity. We're doing this because we know we've got to at least try to bring everyone along.

Is that part of our soul blueprint? Is that part of a soul contract? I got rid of my contracts, so it's not a contract. But something in me is not going to allow leaving behind any stragglers if I can help it.

I'm going to do my best at any rate. That's what resonates with me. Because I do think that the earth is going to go through a major transition that has already begun. As we head more deeply into this transition with the planetary transits signifying great changes and movement upward along with the true advent of the Age of Aquarius, we find ourselves in the midst of a greater awakening than we have ever experienced. The Q phenom was great with people asking questions and realizing that there was a different reality than what they had been experiencing. I've seen, by following the progress, a rise in spirituality and love for humanity. The increase in disclosure will pick up a lot of people, and as these things unfold, I feel that people are being given another chance to opt for the side of light and truth. Without the truth, there is no authenticity. You cannot go through life with blinders on. It's the wrong vibration. You're not going to advance. But you can understand while not letting it affect you.

The terrible things that are going on in the world such as the zombification of people through things like fluoridation, the COVID vax and real life video games in which people are being targeted and hurt, we cannot let affect us. It's a different vibration than the one in which we exist.

You can learn about it, but you can move on from it and keep going and that's where I see a big sweep, where those people who opt for it are going to be moved into the higher dimensions. That doesn't mean picking a side like red or blue or green or yellow.

It means choosing love for humanity over everything else. That's the choice it comes down to. So as I asked in the beginning, what are you going to choose?

We're doing everything we can for us all to move forward as a whole, but there just are some people whose vibration is not able to handle this and who may choose the dark. That's not just about avoiding truth, it's also about attachment to addictions and the more hedonistic things in life, the things that are base vibration and that are hurting themselves and others. It's also about not addressing ego, narcissism, fear complex, or perpetual victimhood. That's choosing the dark.

That's the choice.

Jane: I think that anybody reading this book without a shadow of a doubt, is on this time space reality as a leader of whatever their gifts are and what brings them joy. So we're not actually talking about the people who are reading this book, but the people they love. We're talking about the children we love who are not yet consciously aware of the dark and therefore are still being manipulated by things like mainstream media.

We're talking about friends who are good people, who are kind and compassionate and funny. They are generous or giving and would give you the shirt off their back.

Lane: I would say that by living in compassion they have already chosen.

Jane: We've just had a flood and now many of these people are homeless. They're not vibrating any different to us or we're not vibrating any different to them in those moments. They are all for humanity as they share whatever they've got.

Lane: Those people are going to get swept up in this and come along. The people who won't will likely be the people who have deliberately chosen to stay on the dark side of things.

Jane: I'm not a fan of segregation. The only thing I can see being good about that is if it's vibrational, is that those who have chosen to deliberately and consciously play for the dark, their vibration won't be swept up in this net of going to somewhere fabulous. It's like a cleaning mechanism.

Lane: There doesn't need to be any fear. When someone's holding on to victimhood, for instance, or self pity, or anger, or they commit selfish acts that cause bad things to others unknowingly. It doesn't make them a bad person, but it does mean they're clinging to a darkness.

It's not a matter of being good or bad. It's a matter of making a choice. We've done our best to define that choice, which involves growth into one's true realized self, joy and putting the needs of others into consideration and so forth. It is not trauma based, otherwise you can't get to the point of true unconditional love for yourself and for others.

If you're holding onto trauma, that does not make you a bad person, but you've got to release it, whatever form that takes. Do what you need to do, whether it's psychoanalysis, past life regression therapy, reading books or watching videos on healing your inner child. There's help out there if you want it. You've got to release that trauma because it makes you vulnerable to the dark, in whatever form that may be.

When you haven't healed trauma or addressed your other issues, you're not experiencing what's there for you, that buffet of wonderfulness on the other side.

Chapter 20: Exiting the 3D World

If you make the choice to move ahead the help will be there for you. You will find it. People will spiritually or physically arrive to help you. All you need to do is make the choice. This goes back to polarity and to the old argument: Do we have to have dark because without out it we can't recognize the good?

Where's the contrast? This returns to the choice. For choosing is an active state, while not choosing and remaining in a unknowing state, is generally passive. It comes back to polarity again, where you can't have one without the other.

That means choosing awareness, understanding, and compassion. Those are active states. The question remains: what happens to those around you as you ascend into this new way of being? What if you are lucky enough to throw off the matrix and live in a purely sovereign way of being, what then? Do you become totally out of step with your loved ones? And what of those who say the earth is going to split, or that there will be two earths: will those who don't choose to come along be left behind?

Leaving Others Behind

Jane: I haven't checked out of the system because I have a daughter living in France and I want to get on a plane and go and see her, and there's no way I can travel from Australia to France out of the system.

Lane: When we talked about different states of reality we mentioned how you leave one foot in 3D because we still have to function.

Jane: The way I've reconciled it is that I'm staying within the system so I can do the things that I wish to be doing that are important to me.

Lane: What is the system in this context?

Jane: That's any of their regulation rules, illegal laws, legislation, anything that they tell me that I have to do. Anything that they, being the fat controllers, I mean.

Lane: Yet you were the one in the airport who educated everyone about masks and social distancing as they hauled you off to the clink.

Jane: (laughter) Or tried to. I was going to meet my daughter.

Lane: You chose the very elevated road of refusing to comply and explaining why in a very positive way.

Jane: I pick and choose my battles.

Lane: Yes, because we don't want to be arrested and forced to stop what we're doing if we can help it.

That's having one toe in 3D as I see it, because your children or family are there. We've got people we love who are sewn into the system and we have to allow them their free will. So we're part of the system at times, but yet we can emotionally detach from it.

In other words, we can love and feel empathy for individuals without their experiences having a negative effect on us. We can look at it objectively and understand that it is my free will choice to get on an airplane and go through their rigamarole to see my child in a different country.

I have to comply with their system to do it but it doesn't mean that I am part of that world.

As for the TSA agents who are patting me down because I refuse to go through their Xray machines, I'm laughing with them as they're saying, I have to tap your body like this with these gloves and I say, "I'm grateful for any touch at all." I don't think I've left a single TSA station not laughing. We are one, me and the woman who has to pat me down with her hands up saying, "Okay, I have to do this. It's my job and this is what I'm going to do."

You can get through it if you treat it as an observer. I don't like being routed through crowd control lines, using biometrics, or having my toiletries examined. They threw away the kumquat brandy I brought home from Greece. It was three inches high and tiny and sealed. I asked, "do I really have to throw that out? It is a gift." The agent says, "Well you can go into that area right over there and drink it instead." Being that it was 8 in the morning I returned the bottle and said, "Enjoy it."

People have to participate in the system at times, yet at the same time we're not participating.

Language and Music in Reverse

Our language was reversed. The real languages, Hebrew, Aramaic, Cuneiform, and Sanskrit are of a high vibrational frequency and written right to left. English was created written in the inverse. So we have reverse language designed to entrap us and cut off our frequency.

We also have reverse music, which the Rockefellers changed in the last century to be of a low vibration, throwing world music into a tailspin. The Baroque music and all the wonderful harmonic expression was played in the 432 scale, and then suddenly it all had to be attuned to 440. To push this over the Rockefellers brought in Joseph Goebbels who later became Hitler's PR man.

He's the one who said, "If you tell a lie big enough and keep repeating it, people will eventually come to believe it." Because musicians were revolting against the plan to change the scale of all music, Goebbels was hired to make it appear to be a good thing. The switch from 432 to 440z was enacted and carried into all modern music, where it is designed to lower our vibration.

It is designed to put us in a state of discord and confusion and unlovingness. It's the inverse of the way things are meant to be.

Timelines

I'm going to talk about time and timelines for a moment. What can do your head in is the statement that time isn't linear. Our spiritual mentors say there's no past and no future, only the present. I take this in part to mean there is no past. We're in the moment. If you're thinking about the future, you're not in the moment anymore.

With timelines, you can't think of them literally or in a linear fashion either. We're trying to isolate them but they're intricately interwoven and in constant flux. It helped me to start thinking of them as not as actual timelines, but as states of being. They are trajectories, each with their own outcome. My state of being is that the world is not on a doom timeline. Instead, we are on the timeline in which God wins, love wins, and humanity wins. This timeline state of being is us being here for a jubilant reason, to help push the world into a victorious historical moment where Good finally and forever triumphs over Evil. It's not going *to be*, but *already is* monumental.

We've seen immense shifts occur already, with even greater shifts coming in the near future. The timeline that we are on is of the highest state of being. You can accidentally choose a lower one and go back to all that nasty crapola that the dark side likes to perpetuate. Then you'll need to remind yourself that you didn't choose that timeline. *Say, I don't choose this one. I am on the timeline where good wins.*

Sometimes people in this movement say we've switched timelines again and we're back on the dark one. Maybe people believe we've reverted to the dark one or ones, but I never left the one up top where humanity wins. But there are detours along the way.

A lot of people are leaving the planet now, by choice. They are dying from skyrocketing cancer rates, accidents and suicides. These detours make it appear like the dark has the upper hand.

This does not mean we've left the highest timeline. I think that people get sucked in and take things just too much to heart, or take them too literally. Let's just say we're on the highest timeline where the most glorious outcome is now coming into being.

Jane: I had a very profound vision. I had dropped my husband at work and he unlocked the door to this massive warehouse that houses robotic equipment. As I watched him walk through this tiny door into the huge building I had a vision of timelines as I thought, *I wonder which one he's going into?*

It was like the movie sliding doors where two timelines were playing out at the same time. It's just choices. Then I got that there's an infinite number of timelines for any moment. Any vibrational being has multiple timelines that are happening simultaneously and you jump them by vibration and literally in any moment you have a choice.

Right now I'm sitting here speaking with Lane. Am I choosing to speak about something that is low vibration or something that is high vibration? At the same time that I'm having this very high vibrational, intellectual, emotional, spiritual conversation with Lane, there is also the same conversation going on with Lane at exactly the same point in time space reality where we're talking about low vibrational stuff.

Lane: You just were on to something when you said there are points of connection when you're jumping timelines. That ties into the universe of numbers. There's a scientist by the name of Nassim Haramein who's taken Einstein's theories and progressed them with the 3 6 9 concept that Tesla spoke about. Tesla, you know said 3 6 9 hold the secrets to the universe. Haramein discovered that the toroidal fields that make up the energetic fields of the planet are formed out of 3 6 9, and the intersecting nodes are where humanity has timeline choices. There's your points of divergence, or timeline jumping nodes. There's two toruses, one on top of the other, forming an orb. That's your polarity.

Jane: I think that when we jump timelines some people have the perception that they've gotten off one train and got on another that's let's say, higher and better. That's their perception. But you can keep jumping trains. You can go back to the first train, you can go to this one, you can jump over to this one. It's like we are flying through the air as in dreams of weightlessness where you can scale staircases and mountains.

That's what we're doing. I have dreams where I can run on a hill and then just launch and I fly. I have dreams where I get pulled by magnets up into areas I don't want to be in. That's all we're doing. We're just jumping. When I am sitting here, hoping to write a beautiful book, I am on one timeline.

That is the most highest, purist possibility for humanity. When I jump to a timeline where I connect with somebody I love dearly, they might think that right now Lane and I need to be put into a mental asylum. I jump onto another train and another timeline, and I'm choosing to do that because I want to experience all sorts of things.

I didn't come here to just play nice. I want to get dirty. I want to, dare I say it, have my emotions in all sorts of states of different states. I want the contrast. I want the mud. I want the experiences.

Past Lifetime Polarity

You deliberately uncovered that Atlantis was a past lifetime of yours, Jane. You know that you are here not just to right those wrongs in yourself, but to fix what you did.

Jane: Correct, however, it's all happening simultaneously. There you go, there's the no time, no, no past, no future. This time, am I jumping over to Atlantis and blowing it up? There's a version of me that did do that. Or does do that.

Lane: There's your jumping of timelines, and also time travel. Part of the reason there's no past and no future, is because of time travel.

Now, time travel has become extremely prevalent in our lifetimes. I'm not talking about the concepts of it, but the actual occurrence of it, which is why we have things like the Mandela Effect. This is where things change right under our noses. At one moment Mandela is in jail, at another he is dead. This is because people have come back or people leave. If we're in a time frame of jumping to fix errors of the past then what you just said is absolutely correct. I mean you could be in Atlantis right now fixing what you were or were not doing then. But then what kind of effect does that create? It's a mind bender.

If people are time traveling, and coming back from the future and coming up from the past, then there is absolutely nothing but the present. It's all happening in the present moment.

Just like money, time is not real. As we move into a system where people are finally financially abundant they will suddenly grasp the illusionary nature of money and the complete lack of necessity for it. This mirrors what's happening with time. In this Mandela-like way, as past and future suddenly merge with the present, we're suddenly getting it.

We are suddenly understanding these really difficult concepts. We're seeing examples of things like there is no time, happen before us.

These paradigms we have accepted as true are exploding before our very eyes. Anyone who's saying nothing's happening is completely wrong. It's *all* happening. We're losing illusion on a mass scale, such as the illusion that governments are working for the people.

We're losing the illusion that apathy and inaction is good. We're losing the illusion of complacency. We're losing the illusion that religions are not systems of control. We're losing the illusion that religions are essential, are an essential part of divinity.

All of the false constructs are disappearing, because we're making it happen. Meaning all of us. Because we are opting for the higher timeline, the higher level of ascension, the higher good for humanity, these things are disappearing one by one.

We're literally making it happen.

Trauma Programming

There is one thing I do want to talk about that is not as high vibe as this other stuff. We have talked in the past about energy vampires, about purging them from our lives and not to be one.

We have been in a position where the state itself is an energy vampire where the darkness is co-opting our youth through trafficking and abuse, and also with video games and movements such as climate change, ANTIFA and LGBTQQIP2SAA. I'm not talking about legitimate choices but about getting swept up in movements designed to create separation. That self-righteous separation is co-opting the energy of our youth. The situations in Palestine and all the false flag operations have served as trauma episodes that hit us in the emotional solar plexus. We feel the pain as we watch young children opting for gender surgery and those who regret it later. We feel the pain as the voices of 3000 scientists opposing the legitimacy of climate change are swept under the rug, while slick talking heads talk about the need to eradicate farming. My point is that these things can be very traumatizing if we allow it. These are deliberate attacks on us energetically.

I talked earlier about how MKUltra evolved into a level of programming of the public.

Trauma episodes like 9 11 and the school shootings are here to reprogram us. You can say that this occurs on a physical level to usher in the age of surveillance and eradicate the 2nd Amendment. However here I'm talking about how on an energetic level we are programmed through trauma. This is the real reason why trauma is bad, and why you need to purge it from your life. You cannot allow yourself to be traumatized by the things that happen on this 3D planet because to do so is create a vulnerable state in which you are highly susceptible to programming.

Things can be horrible. I've lost people I love too. But you cannot allow the trauma. I've been wounded in relationships, terribly wounded. I have worked through the trauma. You have to deal with it and purge it. Then forgive it and those who perpetrate it. That moves us into another whole other area, perhaps the most important one of all.

Skyrocketing Through 5D

We need to forgive every single situation. I think that's pretty well known within the community of people who are trying to be the best version if themselves. But, it's not a state of just forgiveness we are looking for, although that's a vital step.

Yes, you also have to be grateful for each and every experience. I mean truly grateful, from the heart. Say it and mean it. Say, *thank you, I'm so glad that I just stepped on that broken glass and it went into my foot because it could have been much worse and I've now learned not to walk barefoot in my garage.*

That's a silly example, but whatever it is you must be grateful for the experience. Not *Oh, shit. I just cut my foot open!* There's a huge difference between those two reactions. No matter what the situation is, you need to be able to see the good in it and be thankful for it. When my father died in the seeming peak of health it was devastating, for we had no expectation of it. However he did not experience the physical decline that so many do at an advanced age. He did not suffer in death and left quickly. Before he died he was writing a book on the meaning of God. Perhaps he is writing this book with me now. I am extremely grateful for the experience of having him as a father for as long as I did, and in good health. I am glad he did not suffer. And I am very grateful for his continued presence.

Moving on from being able to thank the Universe for that experience, we need to love the experience. That's a big leap, but doing this is going to push us right to the top of 5D if not higher. We need to love the experience. Loving it is everything, for all experience is good. There is no such thing as bad karma. There is nothing bad. It is all part of the 3D experience.

I love this life and all its experiences. Happy, sad, tragic—somehow we must get to the other side through gratitude and love.

Loving It

I would like to talk about who we really are and why we came here and how we get caught in this density. That's a whole 'nother line of inquiry. Let's just say that we are the brave ones. Alex Collier talks about this as do a host of researchers.

We are the brave ones. We came down to this planet. We left whatever density, lightness or dimension we were experiencing at the time, and opted to be here. We have had multiple incarnations since. We got stuck in the densities. We ended up doing things that we shouldn't have done, maybe. I don't want to say shouldn't, but let's say we feel badly about having done them.

Jane's Atlantis lifetime, mine where I dumped boiling oil on a loved one's head because that's what the king told me to do—stuff like that. We've been there and got stuck in this 3D vibration. We have fought through it lifetime after lifetime. We have risen steadily. We should be pretty damn proud of ourselves.

The ones on the other planets where we came from, they didn't come, now did they? Where are they? They're in their ships, or here among us and giving us advice. I'm grateful for it, but we're the ones having this 3D experience and we need to take whatever knowledge we receive and apply it through our own lens.

It stinks a lot of the time, but we need to look at the good side. I know that if we do that, we're going to advance right out of this.

The love of the experience came from Nietzsche. He was a stoic, and he figured a few things out. Brilliance comes through different sources, and he's right. You have to love it. How do we do that? My big advice is to laugh yourself silly. Just laugh, laugh, laugh.

My family laughs at funerals. They're renowned for it. It's it's ridiculous, I know. I can't explain it.

Jane: You know how I used to faint at funerals. You laugh, I faint.

Lane: I do go in the bathroom and cry but the larger group learned to laugh. There's funny things in everything. Here's my mom's story. A close aunt had passed, somebody they loved very much. My mother and her brother and sister, in other words my aunt and uncle, went to the wake and greeted apparent relatives they hadn't seen in some time. Typical Italian weeping and wailing filled the viewing room as they move to the side of the coffin. As they look down something hits them. They turn to one another. This wasn't Aunt Tini.

Their laughter came out in fits. Their eyes watered and they shook uncontrollably. Their hilarity grew as they attempted to back out, everyone staring, tears streaming down their faces. They entered the correct wake next door convulsed with laughter.

In hindsight, this was how they dealt with trauma, and it's very effective.

Jane: It is an awful lot of naughty fun to get in a laughing, giggling fit in moments when it's inappropriate, but it's wonderful. Laughter is very powerful.

Lane: I remember being in 11th grade chemistry, when I reached my hand back into my purse. At that age, one had to have lip gloss at all times.

I'm reaching back and accidentally grab Barb Malone's foot. Now, there was no stopping it. I start laughing. She starts laughing. I'm soon hysterical. She's hysterical. My teacher, Mr. Friedman flushed red with exasperation and ordered, "you two, stop it."

We were good students in there. We never got in trouble. This was outside the norm. But he grew beside himself. He didn't know what to do with us because now the whole class was in heaving laughing fits.

He keeps repeating, "You two stop it. You've got to stop it now." The more he says this, the harder we laugh.

At some point he's purple. He says, "That's it. I'm giving you all a quiz on last night's homework." And then the class was mad at us. But once the laughter begins, it just doesn't stop.

Jane: My memory was Brett Marr, an Australian Olympic basketball player. He's a dear friend, and we were sitting side by side at a sports awards night when someone goes to the podium to make his award speech.

Brett leans in and says, count how many times this guy says, "uhm."

Not everybody's the great public speaker Brett is. As the guy starts saying "uhm," I start laughing. I'm trying to fight it. I'm spitting wine through my nose as Brent counts. I'm trying not to snort. "He's up to 80," says Brett under his breath. My attempts to stifle my laughter grew futile. If I hadn't been sitting next to Brett Maher, I would definitely have been thrown out of that dinner.

Chapter 21: Moving Into Mastery

In the community where I moved we have a homeowners association of 18 townhomes. Many of my neighbors are getting on in years. They did not like the HOA president and said that I had to run. I tried to put them off, because the thing I hate most is politics and anything that takes me away from the work that is my passion to do.

After I turned them down, the treasurer died and they looked to me to take the role. I was thinking, there's no way I have the time and energy to learn accounting software and count dollars. Where am I best suited? My skill is in communication and figuring out solutions to problems. It may actually be one of my superpowers. I wouldn't say fix problems, because then you're imposing on other's free will, but rather to find solutions and bring people together.

I said no thank you to the treasury position, I'll be VP. Thank you very much.

Then I went and found tree people to assess a dying tree I thought we could save while somebody else stepped forward to do the number crunching.

Knowing your gifts and how best you can be of service to mankind is part of your path. 15 years ago I made the decision to never attend a demonstration of any kind. Normally I'd be on the front row waving my picket.

This decision came about after I learned they were targeting people. Remember the Tea Party? The demonstrators had their license plates recorded and subsequently had their tax returns flagged. In various demonstrations involving other movements, people have been killed, arrested, and if they are on the wrong end of the political spectrum, have received extended jail terms. Remember Charlene Woodard, the actress who got arrested because she was demonstrating for the pipeline up in the Dakotas? I decided that just wasn't my job. My skills are much better served in other areas. I decided it was not worth putting myself on the front line to possibly be arrested or worse and instead focus on where I can do the most good. It's not just a matter of *know thyself*, it's knowing where your best course of action lies.

The Loaf of Bread

Going back to that loaf of bread and whether you give it away or keep it, I'm wondering if I should keep the bread. In other words should I do everything I can to keep myself alive because I'm trying to help the world? Or do I allow someone else to step into that position? I still don't know the answer to that question, but I guess it's like the airplane-is-going-down scenario where if you don't put the mask on yourself first you can't help anybody else.

My real answer to the bread is to learn to live without food and stare at the sun. In other words, become a breatharian and give your bread away.

Jane: I've actually met a person that lives that way.

Lane: Oh, really? Did it work?

Jane: He joined a dinner club years ago when I was running dinners for single people. I thought *but mate, you don't eat!* I think you might be better off going the cocktail parties.

Lane: Oh, did he drink?

Jane: No, he was into very clean living.

Lane: So no eating or cocktail drinking. Great. I'm just trying to get the rules down.

Taking on Roles

Back to our gifts and how we are best serving. There are times you have to take on roles that do not utilize your skills, but can lead you to the point where your skills will come into play. Through long trial and error, I think I've figured out what I am.

Jane: What is that?

Lane: I think what I am is an alchemist of the soul.

Jane: Yes, absolutely, that's it. 100%.

Lane: What we've been talking about all along is actually the alchemy of souls. Creating the gold within.

Jane: Yes. I think everybody will become a master of some form of self alchemy. Hence why injustice and lack of compassion or elitism, fire you up. They're the same things that fire me up.

Lane: For a long time, I thought I was an energy transmitter. I had a past life in Lemuria where I wore long red robes and stood on a promontory, arms out, transferring energy down to the people. I was a human antennae. Let's say it did not end well because my body was burned from the inside out. The servant who tended me as I died was my daughter in this lifetime.

Before thinking I was an energy transmitter, I thought that I was a conceptualizer who surveyed the world and translated it for humanity. But soul alchemy is where I feel I am today.

Jane: I think I read the collective consciousness. I can read that really well. You read that well too.

Lane: You do read it very well. It isn't so much collective consciousness for me. That is something I evolved into, but I could see the world clearly, I thought, more than others, although not nearly as clearly as I see it now. I could put abstract concepts into words that people could understand, I hoped in an interesting manner. I wanted to bring others to an aware state of doing something, in other words inciting to action. Part of this involved being an energy transmitter, because I knew that's what people needed at the time. A few years ago I was told by my guides not to do that anymore, that I wasn't to burn my insides out anymore.

I've had other lifetimes of sacrifice, particularly one as a gladiator where I fought for the freedom of the slaves, like Spartacus. They recently said I wasn't supposed to do this either.

You don't always know the meanings of all the messages that come to you until time has passed. In pondering that, I realized I was to survive this lifetime and not sacrifice myself. I was here to do a job, but to do my best to stay safe. That's what it means.

Jane: You've made it to this point in this incarnation. It doesn't make any sense for you to be a sacrificial lamb now, no sense whatsoever.

Lane: So do you give the starving person that piece of bread, or do you save yourself if you're here to do something?

Jane: You save yourself. I feel clear on that. It's not it's not an ego or a selfish thing. It's knowing there's a job to be done and it's not saying the other person isn't as important or more important or less important than you, but it is knowing your role to play in this. That must be protected at all costs.

Lane: Yes, that's right. It's not selfishness or service to self, but knowing what needs to be done.

Jane: Now in that same action, you could project your intention for that person to have an effortless process of getting bread from the place next door within the next half an hour.

That's the win. You visually see them thriving.

Intention and Water

Those who are aware have been working with intention for quite a while now. Intention is at the basis of everything, and it begins with your thoughts. Looking into Dr. Masaru Emoto's experiments with water for example, will change your life.

Emoto's groundbreaking experiments demonstrated how water and other substances react to intention. He used words, images and sound and placed them on or near water. In some instances he used labels on a glass of water, such as "beautiful" or "ugly." The effects on the cells are astounding. Under the microscope the cells of the positively labeled water were exquisite. Those subjected to negative words fractured into contorted, blackened formations.

You need to use intention every single moment of your existence. It goes even further than this, for intention is pushing something into the future. Intention is more of a state of gratitude or perpetual appreciation for what is about to occur.

If my intention is to heal myself with this prayer or affirmation, I thank the Universe in advance of that occurring. So my intention is actually grateful appreciation of the act that has already occurred. In this sense there really is no past or future, only the present.

If we look at something as having already occurred, the Universe responds and creates that situation.

If you look at yourself in the morning every day and say, *hello, beautiful*, you're going to be beautiful. If you look at yourself and say, *Oh, I look so old, look at those wrinkles*, things are going to get worse.

Past, Present and Future

Jane: I love that you've mentioned bringing it into a state of it's already having happened. So it's, *I am grateful for my vitality and beauty*. The, *I am* statement is more powerful than the, *I will*.

Lane: The word intention, although it sounds right, is not quite right, because that is pushing the desired outcome into the future. If you're creating a product and the intent is to heal people it's better to move it into the present tense and say, thank you for healing the masses with this product.

Jane: So it's gratitude. Beautiful. Regarding Dr. Emoto's work, I wanted to add that Darren Weissman worked with Dr. Emoto and went on to do the experiments with blood. You can see before and after in his book, *The Power of Infinite Love and Gratitude*. He's got a stack of before and after photos showing intention used on blood work. You can see somebody who's turned up stressed and he's done the blood work before and then after with the power of intention, of infinite love and gratitude.

What has resulted in the blood work after is fabulous. Intention is something that is happening regardless of whether people are aware of it or not.

Meaning, if people are not aware of their thoughts their intentions can harm them. The more that we become consciously aware of our thoughts and redirect them toward the positive, more benefit it is to us.

Lane: Thought is important. We have to start with the thought, then the word, then the deed as it says in the Bible. They got that right. So you have to redirect your thoughts.

Unhijacked Thought

We've been programmed in so many different directions even our thoughts have been hijacked to make us think that we're less than what we are. I'll use age as an example.

My mom never ever wanted her age revealed. Part of that was because she was in the public eye and aware of the prejudices against age, and part of it is because she was 100% correct in knowing that if you thought your age, your body will respond to it. We are conditioned to think that the age of 62 means something, that age 82 means something, that 42 means something, and that 22 means something. Your body responds in kind.

Maybe it was from her, maybe it was my own self, but as a teenager, I never knew my age. People would ask, how old are you? I'd go back to figuring it out and say, Oh, I'm... I'm 16. After a while I stopped doing that and as I eventually grew more fully into myself, I said instead, "I don't do age."

Chapter 22: Unleashing Your Superpowers

Like I said, I don't do age, at least not in the way other people do age. Part of that is because time is a false construct that they've perpetrated on us.

So number one was to trick myself, in a matter of speaking, into believing there was no age and not buying into what age means to other people.

When people say they're going to get old and sick and die and get dementia just like everyone else, they do. That's exactly what happens. In my family no one bought into that. Start by not letting your body buy into the whole what an age means concept. That's step one. The next step is to truly believe that you're 22 in mind and body and spirit or whatever age you feel like being.

Reverse Aging

I never felt like I aged in my thirties or forties. I just never felt it. I'm not saying I look like I'm 22, but I know that when I get pressed to tell people my real age I receive very shocked reactions. There is truth to the adage *you are what you think.*

I've been largely able to master the concept that the age progression program here on earth has nothing to do with me. It has nothing to do with who and what you are. While I do fall into it sometimes, mostly I tend to ignore it.

Jane: That is so unique. I have never heard of another person from such a young age, choosing to not engage in any age dialogue. To not know your age when you were young is extraordinary.

Lane: I have to credit my mom and also I think, because you know I can't do time zones very well. I mean I could, if I really tried, but we both have a problem with grasping this false construct, and it's not because we're less than, or unable to do math, it's because it's not right. If I'm talking to you at the same time, we're in the same energetic zone, so why the difference in time? 6pm or 6am, we're in the same moment. There's something wrong there.

It's the same thing with daylight savings time. It's not correct. When you are inwardly revolting against something, however subtle, you need to pay attention to it. Chances are there's something wrong with the concept you are wrangling with. This is where there's something in your inner self saying, *Hold on. Wait a minute. There's something not right about this whole age progression thing. I am not growing old. I am not growing infirm. I am proactive and not taking bad things into my body. I'm not buying into the medical BS.*

Once you go down the road of tests and specialists, they'll have you believing all sorts of terrible things. Instead, why not stay very in touch with your body so you can read its signals. Part of this is not taking medicines which disguise our body's natural rhythms and responses.

Tuning Out the Negative

Many friends who have had to deal with cancer have received horrible prognoses. The worst thing a doctor can do is to stand by your bed and deliver a terrible outcome. Your first task then becomes not absorbing that prognosis into your cells.

Go back to Dr. Emoto's experiments. We are mostly water. Your body is hearing the words that say you have a 90 percent chance of dying in the next three months, and that while we can put you on an extensive chemotherapy, you're going to die anyway. Your body which is primarily water is hearing that.

That's why I never, ever want to tell anyone my age, because every time you say it, your body hears it and you're thinking it. And those concepts of what age means, however hard you try to ignore them, come into play.

I've done age experiments with my pets. I lived in South Florida for a while, surrounded by older people. Everyone there loved dogs. Mine was a cute little fluffy white guy.

They'd always ask, *Oh, how old is your dog?* And I'd always answer, *he's two.* Somebody would eventually say, *didn't you say that last year? And the year before?*

He was two for ten years, because I didn't want my dog to think he's old. You can say what you will, but animals understand everything. Even if it's not the exact words that they understand, they understand the intent and meaning behind them. They get it when people lean down and say, *oh you poor old thing. Is your eyesight going yet? My dog's eyesight went when he was eight...*

I don't want my pet's cells absorbing that kind of info. I had a dog who lived to 18 who still thought she was a puppy because we always said, "you're a puppy." She was probably thinking, *But I've lost function in my legs. I'd say, it's okay. You're still a puppy.* And I believe she thought she was up until she died.

Jane: I find this fascinating because when I started doing radio I never hid my age and I was really proud when I turned 50. As far as I know, I was the oldest woman in Australia to be given a national radio show. I was proud of that, and I also didn't want to buy into this program of lying about my age and trying to be younger than I am. I wanted to embrace whatever stage I was at. I'm actually really proud that I have never hidden anything like that. But listening to you, I realized I'm still buying into the bullshit. You were at a much, for want of a better word, a much more advanced, higher level of awareness around the age game than I was.

Lane: Maybe I'm just more stubborn. There was a moment

in time where I stood on the precipice, so to speak, thinking, look, I have quite a number of ambitions that I am going to fulfill in the latter part of my life. And maybe it is a good idea to state my age publicly so that women can have this example.

Then as I kept thinking about it I realized that at least for me, the better example would be to demonstrate how to defy age. Like really defy it, if I could do it. Obviously we're all working on different aspects of ourselves, and I'm far from having perfected this. This is what I chose to do.

Grace

Jane: I wanted to talk about grace because over the last three, nearly four years, we've watched a lot of lack of grace, a lot of hostility from all sorts of people. A lack of respect of allowing others points of view.

I think that grace has a big role to play in the coming years. You are very gracious. I've watched you in millions of zoom meetings in varying conversations, and you are the queen of grace.

Lane: Thank you for saying that. My mom taught me about grace. She's a very gracious individual. We would talk about this at the dinner table, being aware that people in our circles did not always have grace. We would examine and ask why someone was so rude or affrontive in their behavior.

Graciousness, I think, is allowing another person the space to have their opinion. When you know more than them, and they don't have all the facts, you can either graciously offer them some of those facts or you can step away, depending on how receptive or unreceptive they are.

Graciousness is courtesy and also kindness. You don't attack. You don't put people down, and you allow them to be who they are. You honor them, even if you think on some level they're not worthy of that honor. Nonetheless you honor them because they are human just like you are, and they have something to offer.

They may not be doing it in the same way as you, or in a way that you personally give a lot of importance to, but you can still be nice in that moment and make them feel good. Everyone. Treat others as you would be treated yourself. Make them feel good about themselves, for isn't that how you want to feel?

Make them feel important, if you want, in some small but significant way. Now I'm not talking about dynamics like women historically being used to prop others up at our own expense. That's a different thing and one that needs changing. I'm talking about daily interactions with anyone, including your partners or family or coworkers, associates and strangers. Make a person feel good about themselves, say something nice but sincere, not, *Oh, what a pretty, red dress*, but something intrinsic to them, like how they wear that red dress. When you do this, you're going to change their lives in the moment.

Jane: That ladies and gentlemen, that is the example of somebody who's done the work, who isn't being triggered, who doesn't need to be heard, seen, felt as the smartest person in the room, even if they are on a particular topic.

And that is grace.

Lane: Wow, thank you.

Jane: But that really is it. You're not triggered. Most people are triggered with, hang on, *I don't agree with that and I need to be heard and seen and felt and validated and I need to convince you all because the world's going to end and blah, blah, blah, blah.* You're just not buying into any of it.

You are vibrationally operating at a very high level where you've gone beyond these things. You choose your intention which is to ensure that you have left somebody feeling better about themselves. If we all master that, we're in heaven.

Lane: I assure you there's no downside to that. It's not lessening you or your worth in any way.

If you're making somebody feel better about themselves, when you point out something you have observed in a person that they haven't recognized themselves and bring it to their attention, it becomes a magical moment. Everyone can do that. You can do a modified version with a person you are only meeting for a moment, like a checkout person or the UPS delivery person. It takes only a moment to really engage with them and give them an honest to goodness thank you. It changes the energy.

Validation

Jane: You touched on an important point. You don't need others to validate yourself. That should be rule Number One on any self mastery journey. Do not look outside yourself for validation.

Lane: Do not! It comes from within. Period. If you look for others to recognize your specific genius or skills, you're going to spend a lot of wasted energy because no one cares. Ultimately, everyone just cares about themselves.

Jane: How do you validate yourself?

Lane: I'm impenetrable.

Jane: I love that. Impenetrable.

Lane: I'm impenetrable because I went through years of rejection. Years where I perfected my skills. Instead of going back and crying I went and made my writing so tight, so over the top airtight that I knew when I had created something worthy. I'm going to sound like an egotist here, but I worked on my skill level in all areas until I got to a point where I am completely confident in what I do. 100%. Having been in the NYC talent agency game, I also know how much of the alleged confirmation of worth you receive is based on opinion and not facts.

I know from being in the media industry, entertainment, alternative news, and all the different fields that I've worked in, that most people don't even know what they're talking about. Some do, but it's a rare thing to run across somebody who actually is at the top of their game and knows what they're doing.

Does that sound horribly egotistical?

Jane: No, because it's a program for us too, the tall poppy syndrome. Cut down ourselves and don't brag. That's a program. The more people who confidently speak like this and shine their light, the more it gives others permission to do the same.

Lane: However if I'm out there in something like a CrossFit class, I know I'm the worst one.

I am 100 percent confident I am making a fool of myself. Certainty works both ways.

On the other hand, I am well aware of who I am and what I'm capable of.

Your Powerful Manifestation Ability

For the second time in maybe a week or two weeks, I manifested something bad. Not terrible, just something not good. I thought it and it happened. The first was a coffee pot. I realized that I have to be careful. These are warnings. The more powerful we become the more careful we need to be.

They're just little things, but they're big. The first was where I was driving down to see my mom. She thought I had her little coffee pot because she just needs one cup, right? I said, all I can find is the big coffee pot for 12 cups in my garage. Do you want that? She said, sure, bring it. And then as I'm collecting it, I'm thinking that if I give this to her I will not have my backup coffee maker because God forbid, something happens and I don't have my coffee in the morning before a meeting.

What happened is I'm making coffee the next morning just before leaving, and my coffee pot breaks. It was so immediate there was just no mistaking it. I realized I had to adjust my thought processes.

The second one also just happened. I have a door from my bedroom leading onto the back deck, which I use constantly to take the dog out. It's lovely out there and I use it all the time.

When the handymen were working here, they could never get the door open, but I always could. I'd touch it and it would fly open, and they'd ask, what did you do?

It was funny. I've been here a year now and I've never had a problem opening the back door. Well, guess what? Yesterday as I'm opening it, I'm thinking perhaps a bit too egotistically, those guys never could get this door open but I always could. Then today, this morning, as I woke up, I could not get the door open.

It is completely jammed. I can't open it. What is that? It's like instant manifestation in the negative.

Jane: if you flip that and you say, okay, I can open the door effortlessly and easily, Are you forcing that thought and therefore it's not manifesting?

Lane: Yes, exactly. Because I did try that. It was the same thing with my finger and the cells. I programmed the arthritis I had in the tip of my middle finger to go away. I hadn't been able to bend that finger for a year. Then, one night as it woke me from the pain, I commanded my cells to heal the finger then and there. I went back to sleep. In the morning I could bend my finger again, and have been able to ever since.

I have not so far succeeded in programming any other part of my body, at least not so obviously as that. I can heal myself quickly most times but it isn't usually so dramatic.

Jane: I've got similar stories of watching what I manifest with my thoughts. Every time I have a bad thought I quickly bring a shield in. So if it does happen, I'm still protected.

Lane: It's fascinating, that instant manifestation. It's been said that manifestation is going to get faster and faster. For me, it works best when it's almost an unconscious thought.

Jane: Yes, when it's not a forced one. It seems very difficult to control every single thought that comes to us but I know that's what we have to do in order to become, crystalline, right?

Your Mighty Self

The pineal gland is located in the center of your head. This tiny gland is known as the seat of the soul. This is where our intuition comes from and our powers of highest connection. The sad truth is that for many it has been shut down, calcified by fluoride and other chemicals. On the other hand, our intuition has been stifled by us thinking it's not important or as valid as analytical thought. Why has there been an assault on our pineals, you might ask? Because they want us dumb and definitely not hooked into our true powers.

What do we do about it?

Keep using your highest sense of discernment. Keep connecting on all levels. If you want to utilize something tactical, then use zeolite or iodine. Edgar Cayce had a version of iodine called Atomodine which you can obtain online. There's an even better way and that is simply telling your pineal to decalcify, and to rely on your heart based intuition at all times.

By using your highest sense of discernment you move beyond even the heart and the head into pure knowing. Now you're working on not just your pineal but you are freeing your entire self from calcification. This is the start of the crystalline state.

This state of being becomes one of pure connectivity. Your cells are upgrading. Your DNA strands are activating. You transcend dimensions and physical and emotional pain. As the density fades away and you grow lighter, you at last remember who you are. You remember why you are here. Here there are no false constructs, no fighting, or harm to innocents. Instead it is a place of joy, receptivity and sharing. The Creator is no longer just a concept, but something you know and feel. Your love for others knows no bounds, and they in turn love you. This is because you have moved into a new way of being, or the crystalline light body.

Afterword

Welcome to the world of independent thinkers. If you haven't already, you're in the process of shedding the programming which tells you how to think, act, and live your life. At the end of this process is complete freedom.

The books which excite you may not conform to an "accepted" way of thinking. The author may have broken through some barriers. A book may be revolutionary in how it changes your thinking.

Join with others who are rebelling against what is wrong in this world by adopting the biggest revolutionary act of all: standing in your own truth and authenticity.

Sign up for Rebel Readerz at https://LaneKeller.com

To contact Jane Donovan:
   https://www.janedonovan.com.au/

I Hope You Enjoyed This

I hope you enjoyed this book and that you found the information presented here valuable. I sincerely hope it has provided enough information to speed you on your journey to a beautiful, blissful life.

    I ask once more for a favor, and that is to take a moment to write an honest, sincere review of this book on Amazon. Reviews help authors like me out more than you can imagine.

    To leave a review, please use one of these links:

My Book

I link doesn't work, copy and paste:

    Amazon.com: RIGHT SIDE UP: How to Stand Upright in an Upside Down World. Spiritual Healing Tools for Manifesting Abundance, Self Empowerment and Personal Growth (Confessions of a Spiritual Rebel, Right Side Up) eBook : Keller, Lane, Donovan, Jane: Kindle Store

    Or search "Lane Keller, Right Side Up, How to Stand Upright in an Upside Down World," on Amazon to find the book then write a couple of quick sentences.

    I truly appreciate your effort!

Confessions of a Spiritual Rebel Series

RIGHT SIDE UP
How to Stand Upright in an Upside Down World. Spiritual Healing Tools for Manifesting Abundance, Self Empowerment and Personal Growth

HOW TO STAND RIGHT SIDE UP
Self Empowerment Workbook

STANDING RIGHT SIDE UP
Having had a Spiritual Awakening are you Ready to Wake Up Your Friends and Family? The Truth of the World in a Concise and Gentle Guide

RISE TO THE NEW PARADIGM: Arcturian Blueprint for Humanity

About the Author

An undeterred seeker of truth who combines a mix of an advanced professional writing career with the development of empowerment strategies, Lane Keller is the voice and motor behind Bright Mind Media and its subsidiary organizations.

Keller writes in many genres including alternative health, the truth of the world, history and politics, the New World Order, personal spirituality, and more. As an experienced public speaker, Keller has spoken out about the subterfuges afflicting our planet on various radio shows and podcasts.

Keller is a true proponent of empowerment from within, believing that the only way for society to break its enslavement is through education and revibration, without dogma, brainwashing, or hero worship. Keller is committed to unleashing humanity from the control system that binds it through education and the lifting of consciousness.

See more at Lanekeller.com

tiktok.com/@rebelreadz
youtube.com/@lanekeller
x.com/rebelreaderz

Other Works by Lane Keller

Some of my work can be found at the following links.

Alice in Pedoland (2 part docuseries)
https://linktr.ee/aliceinpedoland

Lane Explains, Down the Rabbit Hole in Two Minutes
https://linktr.ee/lslaneexplains

Light Your Fire: The Ayurveda Diet for Weight Loss: Boost Metabolism, Regain Health & Lose weight. A unique and simple system based on the ancient science of Ayurveda
https://amzn.to/4b9NNkq

Why Am I Here?: A Concise Guide to Your Purpose and Potential Written with Joyce Keller
https://amzn.to/49TobHr

Tale of Running Bear, A Picture Book for Adult-Minded Young People
https://amzn.to/4b2MuUs

For more of my work please see my website at www.LaneKeller.com

The world is on the brink of change and it requires independent thinkers and those not afraid to speak out. Let's do it together.

Two Gifts from the Author

Now that we've got a good idea of what it means to rise into our true light bodies it's time to receive the *ARCTURIAN BLUEPRINT* which provides direction for humanity as we enter this new paradigm.

Free copy of Arcturian Blueprint:
https://BookHip.com/CRRVLHT

I'd also like to offer you *STANDING RIGHT SIDE UP, The truth of The World in a Concise and Gentle Guide,* which I originally wrote for my children as an introduction to the false reality of this world, as a gift to hand to your own awakening loved ones.

To receive free book:
https://BookHip.com/KMQTQAD

To receive these both in your inbox, please sign up at LaneKeller.com

www.ingramcontent.com/pod-product-compliance
Lightning Source LLC
Chambersburg PA
CBHW070135080526
44586CB00015B/1699